"*Nosh* is beautiful and inspiring, a̲n̲d̲ ̲I̲ ̲l̲o̲v̲e̲ ̲i̲t̲.̲ . . "

author of *The Heart of the Plate: Vegetaria̲n̲ ̲R̲e̲c̲i̲p̲e̲s̲ ̲f̲o̲r̲ ̲a̲ ̲N̲e̲w̲ Generation*

"Having a new look at how vegetables and fruits can work their way into our meals is only gonna make my Seder that much better. What a fantastic book." —Duff Goldman, author and Food Network star

"Micah's plant-forward approach to Jewish food is fresh, vibrant, and full of joy." —Leah Koenig, author of *Portico: Cooking and Feasting in Rome's Jewish Kitchen*

"*Nosh* provides a fresh, colorful, and modern approach to Jewish cooking." —Kim Kushner, author of *Modern Table: Kosher Recipes for Everyday Gatherings*

"No longer do vegetarians have to long for their beloved Jewish favorites. *Nosh* is a true culinary marvel." —Paula Shoyer, author of *The Healthy Jewish kitchen: Fresh, Contemporary Recipes for Every Occasion* and founder of The Kosher Baker

"*Nosh* is an ideal companion for anyone who wants to balance traditional Jewish dishes with a meat-free lifestyle. Siva has the answer for vegan matzo balls, shawarma, gefilte fish, and even pastrami sandwiches." —Shannon Sarna, author of *Modern Jewish Comfort Food: 100 Fresh Recipes for Classic Dishes from Kugel to Kreplach* and editor of The Nosher

"I'm so excited that Micah's book is finally here! She's authentically brought the past alive and created the plant-forward guide to modern Jewish cuisine. From savory to sweet, there's something for everyone to appreciate across the spectrum of Jewish cuisine." —Jamie Geller, celebrity chef, CEO of Kosher Network International, and founder of Jewlish.com

NOSH

NOSH

PLANT-FORWARD RECIPES CELEBRATING MODERN JEWISH CUISINE

MICAH SIVA

THE
collective
BOOK STUDIO

Library of Congress Cataloging-in-Publication Data available.
ISBN: 978-1-68555-327-2
Ebook ISBN: 978-1-68555-915-1
Library of Congress Control Number: 2023906167

Manufactured in China.
10 9 8 7 6 5 4 3

Cover and Interior Design by Rachel Lopez Metzger.

Additional photo credits:
Hannah Lozano Photography: pages 2, 12, 15, 39, 199, 210, 256
Neetu Laddha Photography: pages 29, 30, 33, 34–35, 44–45, 81, 176–177, 223, 224–225

The Collective Book Studio®
Oakland, California
www.thecollectivebook.studio

To those who raised me to be a fierce Jewish food lover:
my mother, Alyson, and
my grandmothers, Eva and Muriel,

and

to the generations I hope to inspire.

CONTENTS

Foreword by Adeena Sussman 11

Noshing Through Tradition 13

Eating "Plant Forward" 16

Shabbat Matrix 28

Holiday & Everyday Menus 31

Jewish Food Glossary 36

Helpful Hints 41

How to Use This Book 46

Breakfast & Brunch

Carrot "Lox" 50

Heart of Palm "Whitefish" Salad 51

Malabi Porridge with Rose Essence, Pomegranate, and Pistachio 53

Apple and Honey Porridge Bowl 54

Lemony Blintzes 56

Halvah Granola 60

Matzo Olive Oil Granola 63

Passover-Friendly All-Year Pancakes 64

Almond Flour Crepes 67

Soups

Chickpea Noodle Vegetable Soup 70

Fennel and Beet Borscht 73

Sweet and Sour Cabbage Soup 74

Yossi's Lemony Lentil Soup 77

Poppy Seed, Potato, and Caramelized Onion Kreplach 78

Turmeric Vegetable Matzo Ball Soup 83

Vegan Matzo Balls 84

Floater Herbed Matzo Balls 85

Salads, Spreads & Sides

Everything Bagel "Fattoush" Salad with Za'atar Cheeseballs 88

Herbed Horseradish Salad 91

Moroccan-Spiced Roasted Carrot and Chickpea Salad 92

Beet and Sumac Salad with Oranges 95

Smashed Cucumber Dill Salad 96

Pomegranate Lentil Tabbouleh 99

Vegan Potato Latkes 100

Crispy Tahdig Rice "Latkes" 105

Creamy Mamaliga 107

Carrot and Parsnip Tzimmes with Dates and Pecans 108

Cast-Iron Potato and Caramelized Onion Kugel 110

Pumpkin Kugel with Pecan Streusel 115

Beet Baba Ghanoush with Pomegranate 116

Smooth and Creamy Hummus, Four Ways 119

Mains

Savory Pulled Mushroom and Tofu "Brisket" 122

Jackfruit and White Bean "Shawarma" 125

Sesame Tofu "Schnitzel" 126

Tempeh and Artichoke "Marbella" 129

Sweet Potato and Sage Vareniki with Hazelnuts 130

Kasha and Mushroom Cabbage Rolls 133

Tahini Mac and Cheese Noodle Kugel 136

Cheesy Jumbo Stuffed Kasha and Shells 138

Spiced Cauliflower Chraime 143

Red Wine–Braised Beets with Creamy Mamaliga 144

Vegan "Gefilte" Cakes 147

Dukkah-Crusted Fried Cauliflower "Steaks" 148

Baked Herby Falafel Balls 151

Hearty Lentil Goulash 152

Tempeh and Bean Cholent 155

Olive, Chickpea, and Zucchini Stew with Preserved Lemons 156

Sabich Grain Bowl with Crispy Chickpeas 158

Celeriac "Pastrami" Sandwich 163

Sweet and Spicy Harissa Hasselback Squash with Chickpeas 165

Chickpea and Olive Shakshuka 169

Za'atar and Feta Khachapuri 170

Confit Tomato, Garlic, and White Beans with Zhoug 174

Baking & Desserts

Kitchen Sink Mandelbrot 178

Mohn (Poppy Seed) Cookies 179

Passover Black and White Cookies 180

Passover Coconut Macaroons 182

Funfetti Hamantaschen 184

Mini Halvah Cakes 187

Salted Chocolate Rugelach 188

Classic Yeasted Sufganiyot 191

Salted Honey Apple Fritters 193

Buckwheat Honey Cake 197

Aunty Ethel's Jammy Apple Cake 198

Olive Oil, Pistachio, and Ricotta Cornmeal Sheet Cake 201

Halvah Pistachio Babka Rolls 202

Vegan Tahini Olive Oil Challah 205

Classic One-Bowl Challah 208

Israeli Everything Pita Bread 212

Sesame Seed Malawach 215

Mini Montreal Bagels 218

Homemade Matzo 222

Cocktails & Beverages

Pomegranate Red Wine Spritzer 226

Apple and Honey Whiskey Sour 227

Olive and Sumac Martini 227

Horseradish Bloody Mary 228

Mulled Manischewitz 229

New York Sour with Red Wine and Pomegranate Molasses 229

Vegan Egg Cream 230

Halvah Milkshake 230

Date Syrup and Hawaij Espresso Martini 231

Essentials

Sauerkraut 234

Quick Pickled Onions 235

Refrigerated Pickled Everything 236

Tahini Sauce 238

Sunflower Tahini 238

Zhoug 239

Sumac Hot Honey 239

Garlic Toum 240

Cashew "Cream Cheese" 240

Manischewitz Blueberry Compote 241

Chia Raspberry Jam 242

Apple and Pear Charoset 242

Hot Mustard 243

Dukkah 243

Quick Mango Amba 244

Shawarma Spice Blend 244

Simple Applesauce 245

Everything Bagel Chili Crisp 245

Everything Bagel Spice 246

Index 248
Measurement Conversion Table 254
Acknowledgments 255
About the Author 256

Foreword by Adeena Sussman

What's so exciting about the world of Jewish food right now is that a wealth of people, perspectives, traditions, and dishes are welcome at the table. It has been inspiring to watch Micah Siva become one of the new voices of Jewish cuisine. They say that youth is often wasted on the young, but not in this case. Over the past ten-plus years, Micah has channeled her seemingly boundless energy, curiosity, knowledge, and talents into forging a very unique culinary path—and she's most graciously invited us along for the ride.

Through her engaging Instagram posts and the many friendships she has made in the Jewish food world, Micah shares a culturally inclusive, plant-based, and most importantly, DELICIOUS take on the foods of her beloved Jewish heritage. These are recipes that not only nod to tradition, but also feel excitingly relevant for home cooks today. Perfect pancakes for every day that also happen to be gluten-free and kosher for Passover? Check check check! Savory Pulled Mushroom and Tofu "Brisket" that would have pride of place on any holiday table—but is also accessible to vegetarians and vegans? Yes, please! Miso-enriched Chickpea Noodle Vegetable Soup that cures anything that ails you and makes you forget you ever needed chicken in a savory broth? I WANT. And so, dear home cook, will you.

In recent years, we've become more attuned to the advantages of a plant-friendly diet, and Micah is here to be your trusted guide—dishes that remind us of the many ports of call where Jewish food has its roots: Africa, the Middle East, Europe, and more. Her warm, welcoming voice, doable recipes, gorgeous photos, and role as culinary cheerleader-in-residence makes all of this food seem incredibly aspirational and at the same time totally possible.

One of the many nice qualities about cooking with Micah is there isn't even a whiff of preachiness or pretension. She makes gentle suggestions for how to live a more plant-based life, but there's no arm-twisting or guilt (Jewish or otherwise). If this is your first ride on the plant-based train, it will be the steam engine to get you going. If you've already hopped on, this book will get you into the first-class car.

Jewish tradition shines when it nods to the past, yet remains relevant to us in the time and place where we live. The blintz filled with creamy cashews and tofu can be satisfying and nostalgic while pleasing both belly and bubbe with one delicious dish. The foods Micah cooked at her grandmother's side are as much an influence as her very modern, fresh approach to cooking, both of which I admire very much. The recipes come together to create something altogether new, altogether appealing, and altogether Micah. So, start exploring these pages and get cooking. Make new memories for your friends and family along the way. Nosh!

Xoxo
Adeena Sussman
Author of *Shabbat: Recipes and Rituals from My Table to Yours*

Noshing Through Tradition

nosh /ˈnɑːʃ/ *verb*
noshes; noshed; noshing
: to eat a snack : MUNCH

To me, food is so much more than what fuels you. It is the accumulation of tradition, culture, stories, and community. Food means family, love, and most of all, community. Through "breaking bread" or *sharing a meal*, there's no better way to connect with those around us.

My grandmother Eva Epstein taught me that love can be shown in many ways, and to win the hearts of the ones you love, you must do so through their stomachs. She taught me that family is built by peering through the oven door, watching over a pot of chicken soup, and sitting around the dinner table. She taught me how to cook a Shabbat dinner, and that a bowl of warm soup could make any country feel like home. She taught me that marriage needs a little sugar and spice, and that some ingredients you just can't measure—you can just feel how much to use.

From a young age, I could be found in the kitchen with my hands in the mixing bowl, eyes fixated on the oven, and staring with wonder at my grandmother as she cooked. To me, she was magic. She would measure using only her hands, tasting raw dough, and smacking her cherry-red lips in delight as she wiped her hands on the apron tied around her neck alongside a string of pearls. Her incessant feeding was her display of love and affection toward us.

My love for cooking was formed by these childhood memories of putting on an apron and hopping on a step stool to cook with the women in my family. From my great-grandparents, who immigrated to North America, to my grandmothers, who were the glue that held their families together, and finally to my own mother, who despite a demanding career always made time for cooking together and forming memories over meals shared.

At nineteen years old, I moved to New York City to attend culinary school (Natural Gourmet Institute, now a subsidiary of I.C.E.), to learn the fundamentals of cooking, with a focus on plant-based, health-supportive cuisine. That's where I learned the ins and outs of flavors, techniques, modifying and writing recipes and, more importantly, that food was destined to be a part of my future career. After completing culinary school, I enrolled in college to pursue a degree in nutrition, with the ultimate goal of becoming a dietitian. Throughout my time in college, I worked as a food product developer, caterer, and anything food related, creating maple syrup–based products, gluten-free baked goods, and vegetable patties for distribution within school systems.

Fast-forward to many moves, a wedding, and a career in nutrition, and I found myself at a fork in the road. As a new expat in London, I had the opportunity to reevaluate my future. While I had very few answers, and even more questions, I knew that it would involve food. I dove headfirst into the field of recipe development, food photography, and digital marketing, working for multinational brands and media conglomerates, but my passion was always rooted in the food I grew up with.

When my grandmother Eva passed (ז״ל), I was living in London and unable to make it back to Canada for her burial and I was beside myself. She was the inspiration for my career and my love for food and a proud supporter of my work. On the day of her burial, I stirred, kneaded, folded, boiled, and fried kreplach, adding my salty tears to the dough as I worked, finding solace in my favorite dish she made.

While the memories of stewing chickens and roasting brisket bring me back to days cooking with my grandmother, my way of eating and my food ethos has adjusted from the Eastern European "meat and potatoes" way of thinking to a plant-forward way of eating that benefits not only our health but also the health of the planet.

As I've outgrown the comfort of my childhood and forged my own path and family, I've looked to Judaism for community, comfort, and cooking to connect with family, new and old. Living in London, my husband, Josh, and I would attend Friday-night Shabbat services, not for the prayers per se, but for the feeling of belonging in our new home. After services, we would go to a wine bar for a little nosh, sharing what we were grateful for that week. While untraditional, it was a turning point in my connection to my heritage; it broke down the barriers of what it *should* look like, which wasn't always feasible, and instead, it was a window into what Shabbat *could* be, a time for reflection with loved ones, with a blessing over wine, grape juice, or water in a wineglass, and the *motzi* over challah, bread, pizza crust, or even a bagel. To me, this was a modern way to incorporate Judaism into my everyday life. I made space to practice in a way that felt sustainable and authentic to our hectic lives.

I hope that this book helps you find a new way to celebrate your heritage, to be unapologetically Jewish while being authentically *you*. I hope that it connects you to Judaism in new and exciting ways and provides you with inspiration to sprinkle a little bit of nosh throughout your everyday life.

With love & bagels,

Micah Siva

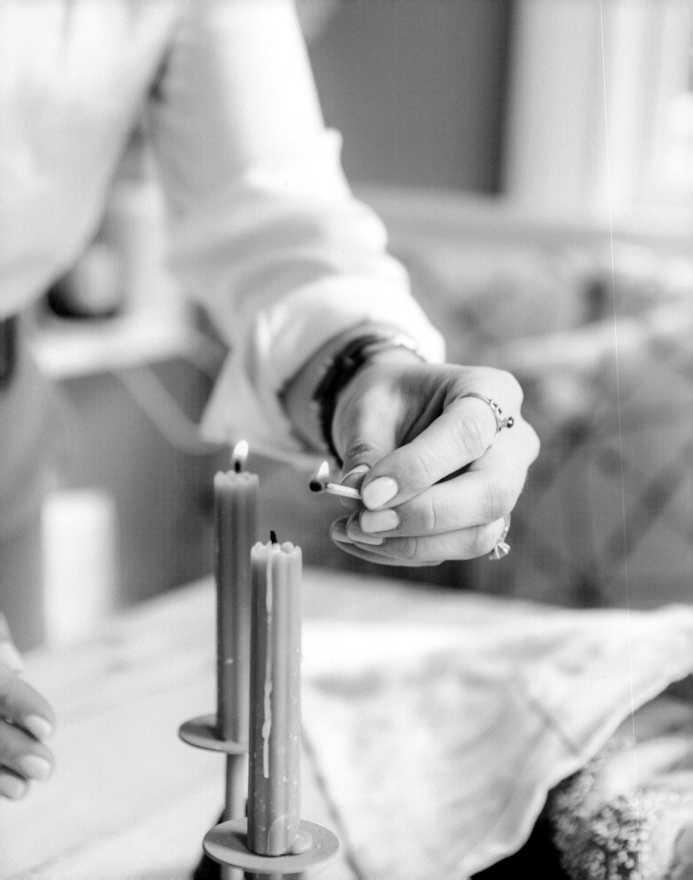

Eating "Plant Forward"

"Plant forward" is a way of cooking and eating that emphasizes plant-based foods without limiting one's diet to being vegetarian or vegan. This book is meant for anyone who follows a plant-based diet or is looking to adopt a plant-forward way of eating.

But How Are You Going to Get Your Protein?

Whether we've asked or been asked this question, it was the main concern for my Jewish Bubbe when I transitioned to a vegetarian diet.

I've purposefully developed recipes that provide whole-food plant protein alternatives to meat protein, from Heart of Palm "Whitefish" Salad using white beans (page 51) to Sesame Tofu "Schnitzel" (page 126). I've also made these recipes ideal for sharing, served as mains, or as an accompaniment to your regular holiday dishes. With many pareve and/or vegan recipes, these can be enjoyed anytime, by anyone, whether they are vegan or meat eaters.

WAYS TO ADD PLANT-BASED PROTEIN TO YOUR FAVORITE DISHES

Beans. Legumes are a quick, easy, and budget-friendly way to incorporate plant-based protein into your meals. Most beans contain around 15 grams of protein per 1 cup of cooked beans, alongside fiber, complex carbohydrates, and iron. I stand behind using canned beans for most dishes. It's simple, time-saving, and doesn't require overnight soaking. The exception is lentils, which don't require soaking, and homemade falafel, which can only be made using dried chickpeas.

Grains. Grains contain 3 to 4 grams of protein per ½ cup of cooked grains; certain grains like quinoa, buckwheat, oats, millet, and barley have more protein than others. As a general rule of thumb, whole grains are higher in protein than refined or processed grains.

Meat Alternatives. With the rise of plant-based diets globally, there are now many meat analogues, including plant-based "chicken," ground "beef," and even fish-free "ahi tuna." Because these products are incredibly brand-dependent and not widely available, I have chosen not to include them in this book. Not only do they differ in quality, texture, and taste, but many of these products are also highly processed and often high in sodium, artificial coloring, and additives. While a plant-based diet can be highly nutritious, a highly processed plant-based diet does not offer the same health benefits.

With that being said, they can be a great addition to your meals on occasion or as a means of using your family recipes and transforming them into meat-free dishes. For example, ground "beef" can be used in your bubbe's recipe for stuffed cabbage, or vegan "chicken" can be added to a vegetable soup.

Nuts and Seeds. Providing protein alongside healthy fats, fiber, vitamins, and minerals, nuts and seeds can be tossed onto a salad or over a finished dish to increase the protein content. When choosing nuts and seeds, look for unsalted, unroasted (raw) varieties. Store nuts and seeds in a cool, dark place to keep them fresh.

Nutritional Yeast. Made from an inactive yeast called *Saccharomyces cerevisiae*, or brewer's yeast, nutritional yeast has gained popularity over the past few years due to its cheesy flavor and nutritional profile. Not only is it a source of protein, but it contains B vitamins and fiber as well. I'm not exaggerating when I say I sprinkle it on everything savory, from popcorn to salads, and it imparts a unique umami flavor. Find it in the health food aisle of your favorite grocery store.

Seitan. Made from the gluten protein of wheat, seitan closely resembles the appearance and texture of meat. Seitan can be easy to find in many grocery stores, but because it is made of wheat, those with gluten sensitivities should avoid it.

Tempeh. Like tofu, tempeh is a soy-based product. Originating in Indonesia, it is made by fermenting a mature soybean cake (don't worry, it is tastier than it sounds!). Stronger in flavor than tofu, tempeh has a texture that makes it ideal as a ground meat substitute. It is a hearty addition to pasta sauces, lasagnas, and stir-fries (such as Tempeh and Bean Cholent, page 155). Because it is a fermented product, it is full of rich umami flavor, but it will still absorb the flavor of your cooking liquid, so you can get creative when you use it.

Tofu. This is one of the most widely available soy products and it comes in many forms, from the soft "silken" variety to extra-firm. It takes on the flavor of whatever you cook it with, so it's ideal to use with a variety of sauces and other ingredients. It can be blended, fried, grilled, poached, or crumbled into dishes for a punch of high-quality protein at a low cost. Tofu can be found in the refrigerated section of most grocery stores.

What About Iron?

Once you get past the protein conversation, you might find yourself fielding questions about iron.

WHAT IS IRON?

Iron is an essential nutrient (meaning our bodies don't make it on their own) that contributes to energy levels, among other things. It can be found in two forms: heme (in animal-based foods) and non-heme (in plant-based foods).

SOURCES OF PLANT-BASED IRON
- Hearts of palm
- Leafy green vegetables

- Legumes (beans, peas, lentils, tofu, and tempeh), with tofu, tempeh, and lentils containing the highest concentration of iron
- Mushrooms
- Nuts, like almonds, cashews, and pine nuts
- Potatoes, especially in potato skins
- Seeds, like pumpkin, sesame, hemp, and flax
- Tomato paste

TIPS FOR INCREASING THE ABSORPTION OF IRON

When compared to heme iron, non-heme iron is not well absorbed by the body, but there are ways to improve the body's ability to absorb this essential nutrient.

1. Eat iron-rich foods with a source of vitamin C.
2. Avoid drinking coffee or tea with iron-rich foods, because it can inhibit the absorption of iron in the body.
3. *Soak dried beans!* When using dried beans, soak them overnight to reduce phytates, which can inhibit the absorption of iron.
4. Cook with a cast-iron pan; while it won't impact absorption, it will impart some iron into the foods.

Substituting Dairy Items to Make It Pareve

When I first removed dairy from my diet, the only options were soy or rice milk...if you could find either. Recently, a surge in plant-based alternatives means that there are countless types of "milk" on store shelves. Whether you are vegan, lactose-intolerant, or looking for a pareve recipe to serve at any meal, you'll find lots of options in this cookbook, including Pumpkin Kugel with Pecan Streusel (page 115), Sweet Potato and Sage Vareniki with Hazelnuts (page 130), and Herbed Horseradish Salad (page 91).

While many recipes in this book are naturally dairy-free, some contain dairy ingredients that are easy to swap for vegan alternatives.

NON-DAIRY MILK

When cooking, it is important to note that the flavor of whatever "milk" you use will affect the flavor of your dish. With that said, I think it's best to always cook with plain, unsweetened milks to prevent a sweet, vanilla-flavored non-dairy milk from ruining a savory soup.

Baking with non-dairy milks is more forgiving than in savory cooking, and most varieties of "milks" can be used in that way. Savory cooking is influenced more by the addition of plant-based milks; the flavors typically come through more. Note that the flavor of the milk should complement the flavors in your dish, and any flavoring or sweetness will affect how it tastes. When adding a non-dairy milk to a savory dish, add it slowly, and mix constantly to prevent separation.

I use only milks I enjoy drinking. If I wouldn't buy it to eat with my cereal, I won't cook with it.

MY TOP MILK SUBSTITUTES

- Almond
- Cashew
- Coconut
- Oat
- Soy

I do not recommend rice milk due to its watery flavor.

BUTTER SUBSTITUTIONS

Chances are, if you keep a kosher home, you are well acquainted with margarine. When I was growing up, our baked goods were always made with pareve margarine so that we could eat them right after any meal.

Coconut Oil. Butter can typically be substituted with coconut oil, but the flavor of coconut will come through. If using coconut oil in recipes for crusts or pastries, be sure to use solid, room-temperature coconut oil, not melted.

Vegetable Oil. Oil can be substituted in a pinch, but the results may differ, especially in baking. A general rule of thumb is to replace ½ cup of butter with ⅓ cup of oil. Be sure to use an oil that you like the flavor of. I love using olive oil or a neutral-flavored avocado oil.

Vegan or Plant Butter. There are some fantastic plant-based butters on the market. When using a plant-based butter for baking, I look for varieties that come in sticks, not tubs. They are often more similar to dairy-based butters, are easier to measure, and work well when baking. All plant-based butters differ in taste, so it may take you time to determine which you like best. My personal favorite is Miyoko's Cultured Vegan Butter.

BUTTERMILK

To make your own vegan buttermilk, add 1 tablespoon of white vinegar or lemon juice to 1 cup of soy milk and mix well. Note that soy milk works best due to its high protein content.

CREAM

If you are looking for a higher-fat non-dairy milk to replace cream or half-and-half, choose canned coconut milk or a plain, non-dairy creamer.

SOUR CREAM OR YOGURT

Look for plain, unsweetened vegan yogurt (I love coconut yogurt) or sour cream (almond- and cashew-based are my favorites). In a pinch, you can use:

- 1 cup coconut cream mixed with ½ teaspoon apple cider vinegar, 2 teaspoons lemon juice, and a pinch of salt
- 1 (12-oz) package silken tofu mixed with 2 tablespoons lemon juice, 1 teaspoon apple cider vinegar, a pinch of salt, and a pinch of sugar

Substitutions for Eggs

Eggs are more challenging to replace than dairy, as the structure and properties of eggs affect not only the taste but also the texture, rise, and overall quality of the final product, particularly in baking. Before choosing an egg substitute, determine what the purpose of the egg in a recipe is. Is it binding? Rise? Tenderness? Not all egg replacements are created equal, so if you aren't sure, you may need to experiment to find the one that works best for you.

AQUAFABA
1 egg = 3 tablespoons aquafaba

If this is your first time hearing about aquafaba, prepare to be amazed! Aquafaba is the liquid in a can of chickpeas or the liquid in the pot after you cook chickpeas. While you may be accustomed to pouring it down the drain, it can be used as a replacement for egg whites; try whipping some up and using it in place of egg whites in recipes like macaroons, pancakes, and meringues! This is used in the Vegan Matzo Balls (page 84).

APPLESAUCE, PUMPKIN PUREE, AND MASHED BANANAS
1 egg = ¼ cup mashed or pureed fruit

To replace eggs, you can use a fruit or vegetable puree. I don't recommend replacing more than two eggs with any of these options, as they impart a lot of moisture and can lead to gummy baked goods. Note that these will also impart flavor and color to your final product, so use sparingly and seasonally!

CHIA SEEDS
1 egg = 1 tablespoon whole chia seeds + 3 tablespoons water

Chia seeds have a unique ability to absorb and retain water. Like flax, chia will form a gel when combined with water, which will act as a binder in your recipe. Chia seeds will be more visible in a recipe and add an appealing little crunch.

FLAX MEAL
1 egg = 1 tablespoon flax meal + 3 tablespoons water

Flax eggs are one of my favorite ways to replace eggs. When flax is mixed with water, it creates a gel-like consistency that can help bind ingredients. Unlike eggs, they do not contribute lift or help with rising. Flax eggs are best used when little to no rising is needed,

such as Kitchen Sink Mandelbrot (page 188), and Vegan Potato Latkes (page 100) and in brownies and cookies. Because of their neutral color and powdery texture, ground flax "eggs" will be nearly invisible in the final product. Be sure to refrigerate ground flax seeds (flax meal) to prevent them from going rancid.

BAKING SODA AND VINEGAR
1 egg = ¼ teaspoon baking soda + 1 tablespoon vinegar

I finally get why this was such an important lesson in my grade-school science class! Not only is baking soda and vinegar an impressive way to make a splash at a science fair, but it is actually a great substitute for eggs. Unlike flax eggs or fruit purees, this alternative can help your baked goods rise. Add an extra ¼ teaspoon of baking soda to your dry ingredients and add 1 tablespoon of white vinegar or lemon juice to your liquid ingredients. I recommend using this substitute alongside one of the other options to both give lift and bind the ingredients together.

SILKEN TOFU
1 egg = ¼ cup silken tofu

For a neutral-tasting egg replacement, try silken tofu. Commonly found in shelf-stable aseptic packaging, silken tofu is a protein-rich egg substitute. It can weigh down your baked goods, so use it sparingly and in recipes that yield a moist bake.

SO...YOU'RE INTERESTED IN GOING VEGETARIAN?

If you are a seasoned vegetarian or looking to decrease your intake of animal products, going cold turkey (pardon the pun) may not lead to long-term success. Here are my top tips for transitioning to a vegetarian diet... and sticking with it.

GO SLOWLY! You don't need to go from zero to one hundred within a day. Take baby steps, and try incorporating one or two meatless days into your weekly routine.

ONE AT A TIME Remove and replace one food at a time. Most people find giving up red meat to be the simplest entry point into plant-based eating. Instead of ground beef in your pasta sauce, try using lentils and/or mushrooms.

CHOOSE WISELY Choose fortified products when possible. If you're replacing your dairy milk with a plant milk, make sure that it is fortified with essential vitamins and minerals.

PLAN AHEAD Vegetarian options and alternatives are all around us, if you know where to look! Planning your weekly meals, lunches, and snacks can help you feel prepared and avoid standing in line for a burger when you've forgotten to pack your lunch.

USE YOUR PANTRY Stock your pantry with protein sources like nuts, seeds, canned beans, bean-based pastas, and nut butters. If you have the elements to make a plant-based meal at home, you're more likely to stick with your vegetarian goals.

GET CREATIVE Try a new recipe once a week. You might be surprised to find some new favorites.

BE GENTLE WITH YOURSELF Most of us were raised on meat and potatoes, and with anything, change takes time!

YOUR PASSOVER KITCHEN

I'm not going to sugarcoat it. Keeping kosher for Passover takes some preparation, whether you are vegetarian or omnivore. You need a basic level of understanding and a lot of cleaning.

During Passover we abstain from eating *chametz* (leaven). We do not eat chametz or grains, such as wheat, rye, spelt, barley, or oats. It is also prohibited for these products to undergo fermentation (see you later, beer) or to have had contact with water or moisture for more than 18 minutes.

Depending on your heritage, your Passover might look different from someone else's. Ashkenazi Jews typically prohibit *kitniyot*, which includes rice, corn, millet, and legumes (beans), as they look too similar to grains. While customarily left out of Passover menus, it is not technically prohibited by the Torah.

Growing up Ashkenazi, we stayed away from both chametz and kitniyot, and after marrying my Sephardic husband, who included kitniyot in his Passover practice, our Passover became a blend of both sides. I still have an internal battle with Jewish guilt when it comes to grains, but we do eat legumes and seeds during Passover.

Many of the Passover-friendly recipes in this cookbook are suitable for Ashkenazi, Sephardic, and Mizrahi. Some recipes use flax seeds, which is widely regarded as kosher for Passover, but you should practice the way you feel most comfortable. It is important to remember that there is no wrong way to practice. Your customs and those of your neighbor may differ, but at the core of our celebrations, we can always agree that food will bring us together.

If a recipe is listed as suitable for Passover, please use your discretion, and do what feels more comfortable for you and your family. The recipes in this book that are "Passover Friendly" will have kitniyot.

WAIT…BUT ISN'T MATZO MADE WITH GRAINS?

Yes. Matzo is made in a highly controlled environment to ensure there is no fermentation or leavening taking place. The process of making matzo is supervised to be within the 18-minute window, to prevent any fermentation from occurring.

WHAT ABOUT BAKING POWDER AND BAKING SODA?

Unlike yeast, baking powder and baking soda rise chemically and do not ferment, meaning they are permissible during Passover. Be sure to look for kosher-for-Passover baking powder and baking soda (typical baking powder contains cornstarch).

FLAX AND CHIA SEEDS

Chia seeds are not considered kitniyot and are suitable for Passover in many cases. Kitniyot is not clear across the board, but many consider whole flax seeds suitable for Passover. In this case, Passover recipes using flax seeds should start with whole flax seeds and incorporate them by grinding them until powdered.

Shabbat Matrix

For many people, the idea of a weekly Shabbat can feel daunting between work, kids, cleaning, and everything else we do. To satisfy my desire to unplug and enjoy Shabbat dinner, I've created this matrix, a choose-your-own-adventure of doing Shabbat.

NOSHING THROUGH TRADITION

LOW EFFORT ———————————————————————————— **HIGH EFFORT**

LOTS OF TIME

- Store-bought pizza dough (braided and baked), wine, and Shabbat candles
- Chickpea noodle soup, store-bought challah, wine, and candles

- Homemade challah, wine spritzers, and hand-dipped candles (or not)
- Homemade challah, wine, and Shabbat candles

MORE TIME

- Store-bought challah, wine, and Shabbat candles

- Frozen pre-made challah (bake), wine, and candles
- Challah from a local bakery, wine, and candles

LITTLE TIME

- Bread, grape juice, and a tea light
- Bread with butter, grape juice in a wineglass, and a scented candle
- Takeout pizza, wine, and scented candles

- Store-bought challah (made into French toast), wine, and candles

LOW EFFORT ———————————————————————————— **HIGH EFFORT**

Holiday & Everyday Menus

ROSH HASHANAH
Vegan Tahini Olive Oil Challah, page 205

Carrot and Parsnip Tzimmes with Dates and Pecans, page 108

Beet and Sumac Salad with Oranges, page 95

Tempeh and Artichoke "Marbella," page 129

Aunty Ethel's Jammy Apple Cake, page 198

Salted Honey Apple Fritters, page 193

YOM KIPPUR BREAK-FAST
Mini Montreal Bagels, page 218

Heart of Palm "Whitefish" Salad, page 51

Carrot "Lox," page 50

Cashew "Cream Cheese," page 240

Lemony Blintzes, page 56

WINTRY HANUKKAH
Vegan Potato Latkes, page 100

Simple Applesauce, page 245

Crispy Tahdig Rice "Latkes," page 105

Savory Pulled Mushroom and Tofu "Brisket," page 122

Smashed Cucumber Dill Salad, page 96

Classic Yeasted Sufganiyot, page 191

HEARTY PASSOVER SEDER
Turmeric Vegetable Matzo Ball Soup, page 83

Vegan "Gefilte" Cakes, page 147

Spiced Cauliflower Chraime, page 143

Herbed Horseradish Salad, page 91

Cast-Iron Potato and Caramelized Onion Kugel, page 110

Passover Black and White Cookies, page 180

Passover Coconut Macaroons, page 182

AUTUMN SHABBAT DINNER

Red Wine–Braised Beets with Creamy Mamaliga, page 144
Pumpkin Kugel with Pecan Streusel, page 115
Herbed Horseradish Salad, page 91
Vegan Tahini Olive Oil Challah, page 205

WINTER SHABBAT DINNER

Tempeh and Bean Cholent, page 155
Everything Bagel "Fattoush" Salad with Za'atar Cheeseballs, page 88
Classic One-Bowl Challah, page 208

SPRING SHABBAT DINNER

Confit Tomato, Garlic, and White Beans with Zhoug, page 174
Vegan Tahini Olive Oil Challah, page 205
Green Salad

SUMMER SHABBAT DINNER

Smooth and Creamy Hummus, Four Ways, page 119
Baked Herby Falafel Balls, page 151
Israeli Everything Pita Bread, page 212
Pomegranate Lentil Tabbouleh, page 99

Jewish Food Glossary

Jewish cuisine and vocabulary are shaped by centuries of displacement, movement, and survival across the Diaspora. There's no one singular Jewish cuisine, and all the varieties have been influenced by persecution, poverty, celebration, and tradition.

Whether this is your first time trying Jewish cuisine or you've been cooking Jewish food for decades, with a culinary history as rich as Jewish cuisine, there are always words, phrases, and dishes to learn.

Amba A tangy, spicy, pickled mango-based condiment or sauce of Indian-Jewish origin. Iraqi-Jewish immigrants brought it to Israel in the 1950s, and it is commonly served with sabich, a common Shabbat morning meal (see Quick Mango Amba, page 244).

Appetizing This is often in reference to Ashkenazi cuisine and generally means "things that go on bagels." It is common to break-fast with a spread of appetizing, as you load up on bagels, smoked fish, and schmear.

Ashkenazi A Jewish person of Eastern European descent.

Bissel or bisl A Yiddish word for "a little bit," often referred to in cooking, such as "Add a bisl of salt."

Blintz A rolled, thin pancake, traditionally filled with sweet cheese and either fried or baked (see Lemony Blintzes, page 56).

Chag Sameach A Hebrew term for "happy holiday," which is customarily said at Jewish holidays.

Chametz A food product made of wheat, barley, rye, spelt, or oats that has come into contact with water and started the fermentation process. Chametz is prohibited during Passover.

Charoset or haroset Stemming from the Hebrew word for "clay," it is a sweet relish-style condiment traditionally made with walnuts, dates, apples, pears, raisins, red wine, pine nuts, cinnamon, and/or sesame seeds.

Cholent A Shabbat dish made of slow-cooked meats and vegetables. It is customarily prepared on Friday and cooked at a low temperature overnight to enjoy on Saturday to comply with the Sabbath laws that prohibit cooking (see Tempeh and Bean Cholent, page 155).

Chraime A spicy North African tomato-based stew customarily made with fish that is typically eaten on Friday evenings (Erev Shabbat), Rosh Hashanah, and Passover. It is popular in Sephardi cuisine (see Spiced Cauliflower Chraime, page 143).

Diaspora The dispersion of peoples from their homeland, which commonly refers to Jews living outside of Israel.

Dukkah or Duqqa An Egyptian/Middle Eastern nut-based condiment made of nuts, seeds, herbs, and spices. It is commonly mixed with olive oil as a dip for breads or vegetables. A little salty, nutty, spicy, and toasty, dukkah blends vary from one to another (see Dukkah, page 243).

Goulash A Hungarian soup or stew that is flavored with Hungarian paprika. It is often prepared with beef, vegetables, garlic, tomatoes, and potatoes (see Hearty Lentil Goulash, page 152).

Halvah A sweet confection made of sesame butter and sugar. It can be flavored with nuts, cocoa powder, vanilla, and rose water, among others. Tahini (sesame) halvah often comes in slabs or "cakes" and is cut into slices by weight. Israeli-style halvah may contain soapwort, a natural plant-based emulsifier that creates a smoother halvah. Halvah can also be made using sunflower seeds, which is common in Eastern European countries.

Harissa A Tunisian spice mix or paste made of dried chili peppers, cumin, coriander, and garlic, among other ingredients.

Kasha These are roasted buckwheat groats. Kasha can be cooked like porridge and is a common ingredient in Ashkenazi dishes.

Kreplach Square or triangular dumplings filled with meat or potatoes and typically boiled or fried. They are often served in soup or with onions. The word comes from the Yiddish *kreplech*, which translates to "meat dumpling."

Kugel At its simplest, kugel is a baked casserole with starch. It is commonly made using egg noodles (lokshen kugel) or potatoes. Kugel is often served at Jewish holidays or on Shabbat. There are three kugels in this book, Cast-Iron Potato and Caramelized Onion Kugel (page 110), Pumpkin Kugel with Pecan Streusel (page 115), and Tahini Mac and Cheese Noodle Kugel (page 136). Give one a try!

Labneh A soft, strained yogurt cheese from the Middle East. The process of straining removes the whey, resulting in a thicker-than-yogurt cheese with a tangy taste.

Lox Lox is a salt-brine-cured unsmoked salmon. Nova lox is cured in a mild brine and cold-smoked. Gravlax is unsmoked and dry-cured. For a plant-based lox, try Carrot "Lox" (page 50).

Malabi A classic Israeli dessert pudding made of rice, sugar, milk, semolina (or cornstarch), rose water, and a sweet raspberry topping. It is thought to have originated in Turkey.

Malawach This is a flatbread in Yemenite Jewish (Mizrahi) cuisine. Cooked in a skillet, its thin layers are brushed with oil, resulting in a flaky flatbread.

Mamaliga In traditional Romanian cuisine, this is a yellow corn porridge. It was commonly known as peasant food when wheat was too expensive for farmers to buy.

Mandelbrot or Mandel Bread The word *mandelbrot* literally means "almond bread" in Yiddish and German. Mandelbrot are crispy, twice-baked cookies, similar to biscotti. They are made with more fat than biscotti, making them richer and less dry than their Italian counterparts. Crispy, crunchy, and flavored with nuts, seeds, and spices, they are often tossed in cinnamon-sugar. In my family, we call it *kamishbrot*, which reflects our Ukrainian heritage.

Matzo Brei A common Passover breakfast dish made of eggs or milk and matzo, fried in butter or oil. The word *brei* means "to sear." In my family, we call it *gefrishte matzo*.

Mizrahi Mizrahi Jews are largely from Middle Eastern heritage with roots in places like Yemen, Iraq, and Iran.

Nosh A Yiddish word for "to snack."

Pareve A dish prepared without meat or milk that can be eaten with both meat and dairy dishes.

Sabich A pita sandwich with fried eggplant, chopped salad, hard-boiled eggs, amba, and tahini sauce. Sabich was brought by Iraqi Jews to Israel. It is customarily eaten on Saturday mornings and prepared the day before. For an alternative, try my Sabich Grain Bowl with Crispy Chickpeas (page 158).

Schmear A Yiddish word for a spread, often referring to cream cheese.

Schnitzel A thin slice of veal or meat that is coated in breadcrumbs and fried.

Seder A Jewish ceremonial dinner, often referring to the first two nights of Passover.

Sephardic or Sephardi Sephardic Jews descend from Iberian Jews who were expelled from Spain and Portugal. It commonly refers to Jews of Spanish or North African heritage.

Sufganiyot (or sufganiyah, for singular) Israeli yeasted jelly donuts, typically eaten during Hanukkah. Try the Classic Yeasted Sufganiyot (page 191).

Sumac A Middle Eastern spice, made from dried and ground sumac berries. It has a tangy, lemony flavor and is deep red in color. In Roman times, sumac was used in dishes to impart a tangy flavor before lemons were introduced.

Tahini Ground sesame paste.

Toum A garlic sauce, similar to aioli, made of garlic, oil, salt, and lemon juice. Unlike aioli, where the egg acts as an emulsifying agent, toum relies on garlic to do so.

Tzimmes Yiddish for "a big fuss," it is an Ashkenazi dish of carrots, root vegetables, and dried fruits with honey (see Carrot and Parsnip Tzimmes with Dates and Pecans, page 108).

Yiddish A Jewish language popular in Central and Eastern Europe prior to the 1930s. Originally a German dialect with Hebrew influences.

Za'atar An herb blend made of sesame seeds, sumac, salt, oregano, thyme, and marjoram. It is a zesty, crunchy, and herbaceous blend that is widely used in Middle Eastern cuisine.

Zhoug or Zhug A bright Middle Eastern condiment, similar to chimichurri or salsa verde. Made up of fresh herbs, usually cilantro and parsley, hot peppers, coriander, garlic, spices, and olive oil.

Helpful Hints

Measuring Flour. Don't scoop up flour using your measuring cup! To accurately measure flour, use a spoon to scoop up the flour and put into a dry measuring cup. Level it with a butter knife.

Measuring Liquids. Place a liquid measuring cup on the counter and look at it from eye level as you pour in your ingredient. The top of the liquid bows slightly. The bottom of the bow should be in line with the measure you're looking for.

Adjusting for High-Altitude Baking. These recipes were tested at nearly sea level and changes in altitude may change the result, depending on the recipe you make. If you live in a high-altitude area, you can help make them more consistently using these adjustments:

OVEN TEMPERATURE: Increase the oven temperature by 15°F or 20°F.

BAKING TIME: Decrease the baking time by 5 minutes for every 30 minutes called for in the recipe.

SUGAR: Decrease the amount by approximately 1 tablespoon for every 1 cup called for in the recipe.

LIQUID: Increase the liquid in baking recipes by approximately 1 tablespoon per 1 cup called for in the recipe.

Choosing Non-Dairy Milk. For most recipes, any non-dairy milk can be used. Choose a plain, unsweetened "milk" for best results. See Substituting Dairy Items to Make It Pareve on page 20.

Knowing When Bread Is Done. The most accurate way to tell whether your bread is done is by inserting a thermometer into the loaf after pulling it out of the oven; the bread is done when the thermometer reaches 190°F. Another way is by look and feel. The bread will be deep golden in color, and when you "knock" on the bottom of the loaf, it should sound hollow.

Choosing Tofu. Tofu can be found in the refrigerated section of most grocery stores. Silken tofu, which is commonly found in aseptic packaging and is shelf-stable, is often found on store shelves in the Asian or "ethnic" food section, or with tofu in the refrigerated section. Tofu ranges from silken, which is the softest, to extra-firm. Recipes indicate which variety you will need, and they are not interchangeable.

Draining Tofu. To use tofu in a recipe, it's best to drain the liquid before using. Some recipes call for pressing the tofu to remove excess liquid. To do this, layer eight to ten pieces of paper towel on a plate. Place the tofu on top, and place another eight to ten pieces of paper towel over it. Top with a sturdy plate and a couple of cookbooks. Let sit for 20 to 30 minutes.

Choosing Canned Beans. This is one of my favorite kitchen shortcuts. When buying beans, I choose low-sodium or no-salt-added beans so that I can control the amount of salt in the recipe. If you can't find low-sodium canned beans and want to decrease the amount of salt in a dish, you can rinse the beans in a colander under cold water for 30 seconds.

Making a Vegan Egg. If you are looking for a vegan alternative for eggs, there are multiple ways to substitute with minimal changes in the final product. See Substitutions for Eggs on page 22.

Melting Chocolate. The easiest way to melt chocolate is in the microwave. Add your chocolate to a microwave-safe bowl and microwave in 30-second increments, stirring at each increment until melted.

Fixing Grainy Melted Chocolate. Melted chocolate becomes grainy when moisture gets in the bowl. Unfortunately, there is no coming back from that. While it may not be good for dipping or drizzling, don't throw it away! You can use it in brownies or cookies.

Making Sure Yeast Is Fresh. Yeast can expire and become inactive, which results in bread that won't rise. You can "prove" that your yeast is active by first checking the expiration date on the packaging and making sure it has been stored properly. Add the amount of yeast called for in your recipe to a bowl and add the required water and sugar or sweetener per the recipe. Let sit for 5 to 8 minutes in a warm place. The yeast should become foamy and/or bubble, which is called "bloom." If it does not bloom or change in appearance, you may need fresher yeast.

Storing Yeast. Single packets of yeast can be stored in a cool, dark pantry. Larger containers of yeast can be stored in an airtight container in the fridge or freezer.

Halving or Doubling Recipes. In many cases, you can halve or double a recipe. When changing the quantity of a recipe, you may need to adjust the cooking time and certain spices, like salt. Before doubling the salt, if possible, taste the dish and add more salt as desired. Please note that changing and/or modifying recipes may change the outcome.

Washing Produce. Washing produce can be done with commercial produce-cleaning products, or you can soak most produce items in a bath of water with a splash of apple cider vinegar.

Fixing an Oversalted Dish. If you've added too much salt in a soup, add a raw, halved potato. The potato will absorb excess salt. Before serving, remove the potato. If it is still too salty, add a squeeze of lemon juice or add more water.

Keeping Herbs Fresh. Many of the recipes use fresh herbs, which I always keep in the fridge. To keep herbs fresher longer, place them in a drinking glass or jar with 2 inches of water and store upright in the fridge or on the counter as you would flowers.

Reducing Food Waste. Once you start keeping track of your own food waste, you'll be surprised to see how much you amass. I try to reduce my food waste in bite-size ways not only to benefit the planet but also to make a positive impact on my grocery bill. I've learned some tips and tricks along the way to make reducing my waste sustainable as well as enjoyable (just check out the carrot-top pesto in my freezer!).

- Keep vegetable scraps in a zip-top bag in the freezer and use them to make stock or vegetable broth.

- Before shopping, take stock of what you have in the cupboard, fridge, freezer, and pantry, so you don't purchase food items you already have.

- In our house, once a week, we have what we call a "triage," meaning we eat up everything that is on its last legs. It often turns into a loaded veggie stir-fry with leftover grains, and it's a good way to reduce waste.

- Learn to preserve! Pickle, jam, or kraut your wilting vegetables.

- Freeze fruit in zip-top bags and add them to smoothies during the week.

- Understand expiration dates and "best before" dates. "Sell by" and "best before" dates don't mean that the food is no longer safe to consume. Always check with sight, smell, and taste to ensure it is still good to go.

Choosing Olive Oil. Extra-virgin olive oil is my go-to oil for 90 percent of my cooking. I use it in salad dressings, to sauté, and in baking. Olive oil is susceptible to damage from light and heat, so I always buy it in a dark glass or opaque bottle. Olive oils in clear glass bottles can go rancid quickly. Stay away from "light" olive oil. It is simply refined oil that no longer has the flavor or aroma of olive oil.

Choosing Nut Butters. The recipes in this book all use natural nut butters made with just nuts and salt. They have not been tested using peanut butter spreads, which generally have sugar and other ingredients added.

Choosing Salt. I typically use sea salt or kosher salt in cooking. If using kosher salt, Diamond Crystal Kosher Salt is the gold standard. When using salt to finish a dish, like sprinkling onto Sesame Tofu "Schnitzel" (page 126), I like to use a flaky finishing salt, like Maldon.

Why Is My Baked Good Darker/Lighter/ Different Than Yours? Baking is a science and even if we stood side by side in the same kitchen, our finished products would have variations beyond our control. The temperature of ingredients, weights, and even the baking dishes we use will impact the final product. My tip? Manage expectations when it comes to baking, and do your best. And just because it looks different doesn't mean it won't taste great.

How to Use This Book

SERVINGS

This is the average serving size, but it will depend on the other dishes you are serving. Use your best judgment; if you are making three different salad recipes for dinner, err on the side of caution, but if you are serving a heartier main dish (like Hearty Lentil Goulash, page 152), you'll probably want your side dish portions to be smaller.

ON THE TABLE IN...

Cooking time is subjective; use this as a guide, as your experience will impact the time it takes to make these dishes.

This is the total time it will take to get your dish ready, including any resting time. In some cases you'll see the addition of "including (a certain amount of) resting time," so you'll be able to see that even if it takes a long time to get the dish on the dinner table, much of that time will be inactive and you can be doing something else while you wait. This could include the time it takes for marinating, letting dough rise, or letting a dish rest.

DIETARY LABELS

The following icons are used in the recipes to indicate whether a dish is gluten-free, vegan, dairy-free, contains eggs, or is Passover-friendly:

 Vegan

 Contains egg

 Contains dairy

 Gluten-free

 Passover-friendly *this indicates chametz-free recipes, but may include kitniyot like chickpeas or legumes, or baking powder. Use passover-friendly baking powder, if preferred.*

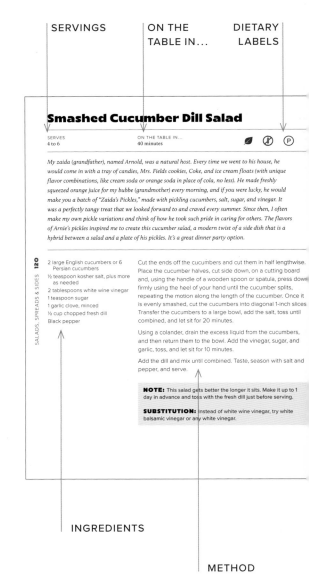

SERVINGS   ON THE TABLE IN...   DIETARY LABELS

Smashed Cucumber Dill Salad

SERVES
4 to 6

ON THE TABLE IN...
40 minutes

My zaida (grandfather), named Arnold, was a natural host. Every time we went to his house, he would come in with a tray of candies, Mrs. Fields cookies, Coke, and ice cream floats (with unique flavor combinations, like cream soda or orange soda in place of cola, no less). He made freshly squeezed orange juice for my bubbe (grandmother) every morning, and if you were lucky, he would make you a batch of "Zaida's Pickles," made with pickling cucumbers, salt, sugar, and vinegar. It was a perfectly tangy treat that we looked forward to and craved every summer. Since then, I often make my own pickle variations and think of how he took such pride in caring for others. The flavors of Arnie's pickles inspired me to create this cucumber salad, a modern twist of a side dish that is a hybrid between a salad and a plate of his pickles. It's a great dinner party option.

2 large English cucumbers or 6 Persian cucumbers
½ teaspoon kosher salt, plus more as needed
2 tablespoons white wine vinegar
1 teaspoon sugar
1 garlic clove, minced
½ cup chopped fresh dill
Black pepper

Cut the ends off the cucumbers and cut them in half lengthwise. Place the cucumber halves, cut side down, on a cutting board and, using the handle of a wooden spoon or spatula, press down firmly using the heel of your hand until the cucumber splits, repeating the motion along the length of the cucumber. Once it is evenly smashed, cut the cucumbers into diagonal 1-inch slices Transfer the cucumbers to a large bowl, add the salt, toss until combined, and let sit for 20 minutes.

Using a colander, drain the excess liquid from the cucumbers, and then return them to the bowl. Add the vinegar, sugar, and garlic, toss, and let sit for 10 minutes.

Add the dill and mix until combined. Taste, season with salt and pepper, and serve.

NOTE: This salad gets better the longer it sits. Make it up to 1 day in advance and toss with the fresh dill just before serving.

SUBSTITUTION: Instead of white wine vinegar, try white balsamic vinegar or any white vinegar.

INGREDIENTS

METHOD

SALADS, SPREADS & SIDES **120**

PICKLES AND JEWISH CUISINE Pickles play an important part in Jewish cuisine, especially for those living in Poland, Ukraine, Lithuania, and Russia. Before refrigeration was possible, pickling was a way to preserve fruits and vegetables to ensure there was enough to eat throughout the cold winter months. There are two main types of pickling: with a brine and with vinegar. Salt-brined pickles are what we now associate with Jewish delis because vinegar was expensive for poor Jews to afford. Jewish home cooks used salt to preserve the summer's bounty along with garlic and dill and were then left to ferment for weeks, if not months.

INGREDIENTS

In every recipe, ingredients are listed in the order of use, which will help keep you organized and ready for the next step. If a *comma* is used in the ingredient list and is placed *after* the named ingredient, measure the ingredient prior to prepping. For example, "1 cup walnuts, chopped" means you should measure out 1 cup of walnuts and then chop them. If it calls for "1 cup chopped walnuts," you should chop the walnuts first and then measure them.

METHOD

Before starting a recipe, review it and read the directions; some recipes require soaking, resting, or rising. No one wants to wait 4 hours for a dish they had planned to eat *now*. Knowing when and what you need to do will help simplify the process.

UNDERSTAND THAT RECIPES ARE GUIDES

When it comes to your kitchen, you're in charge. If you don't like certain ingredients, substitute another. If you can't stand cilantro, use parsley or fresh mint. Recipes are guidelines, not hard-and-fast rules. Have fun with it! I find joy in riffing a little off of tried-and-true recipes and adding my own unique spin on the classics.

Breakfast
& Brunch

Carrot "Lox"

SERVES
6

ON THE TABLE IN...
1½ hours, including 1 hour of resting

Nothing says Jewish food more than bagels and lox. It's the unofficial dish of every oneg (luncheon after synagogue services) and is a staple on deli menus across America. This recipe for carrot "lox" is full of smoky flavor thanks to liquid smoke, with a touch of sweetness from maple syrup and briny nori seaweed to achieve a fishy taste. If you don't eat fish, there's no reason to miss out on the rich, salty, and smoky bagel topping.

3 large carrots, scrubbed

3 tablespoons liquid smoke

1 tablespoon maple syrup

2 tablespoons extra-virgin olive oil

1 tablespoon lemon juice

¾ cup water

½ teaspoon sea salt

¼ teaspoon black pepper

2 (8-by-7-inch) sheets nori, roughly torn into 4 to 6 pieces

Using a vegetable peeler, peel the carrots into long ribbons. Note: Apply more pressure for thicker ribbons.

In a medium saucepan over medium heat, combine the carrots, liquid smoke, maple syrup, olive oil, lemon juice, water, salt, black pepper, and torn nori sheets and bring to a boil. Lower the heat to a simmer, and cook until the carrot ribbons are tender, 8 to 10 minutes.

Remove the pan from the heat, cover, and let sit for 20 minutes to cool. Transfer the carrots, liquid, and nori to an airtight container, place in the fridge, and let marinate for at least 1 hour before serving.

When ready to eat, add the carrots to toasted bagels with Cashew "Cream Cheese" (page 240), fresh dill, red onion, capers, cucumber, and tomato. Or add your carrot "lox" to a vegan brunch board.

WHAT IS LIQUID SMOKE? One of my secret ingredients in this recipe is liquid smoke. It is a natural by-product of burning wood; the smoke is distilled and concentrated into a liquid. You can typically find liquid smoke near the barbecue sauce in your local supermarket. Store liquid smoke in the pantry for up to 2 years.

NOTES: This fish-free recipe will last up to 1 week in the fridge. Keep the carrot ribbons submerged in the smoky brine and the flavor will deepen over time! To enjoy, drain and add to bagels, sandwiches, and salads.

Heart of Palm "Whitefish" Salad

SERVES
4

ON THE TABLE IN...
10 minutes

There's something special about smoked whitefish salad, a dish that is rarely seen outside of Jewish delis. Made with mayonnaise and sour cream, smoked whitefish, fresh dill, and lemon, it is commonly served at shiva, break-fast, or post-synagogue kiddush. This vegan take on the classic uses hearts of palm and creamy white beans to replicate the rich and flaky texture of whitefish. Flavored with vegan mayonnaise, lemon zest, Dijon, and salty dulse (seaweed flakes), this "whitefish" salad is delicious on bagels and breads or served in a scoop on top of a salad.

In a medium bowl, roughly mash the beans with a fork. Using a fork, shred the hearts of palm into the bowl with the beans. Add the celery, red onion, mayonnaise, Dijon mustard, liquid smoke, lemon zest, dulse flakes, lemon juice, and 2 tablespoons of the dill and mix until well combined. Season with salt and pepper, to taste.

Top with the remaining 1 tablespoon of dill and serve immediately.

NOTE: Store in an airtight container in the fridge for up to 4 days.

VARIATION: Try using canned artichoke hearts in brine or jackfruit instead of the hearts of palm.

SUBSTITUTION: Use 1 teaspoon of finely chopped nori seaweed for the dulse flakes or simply omit it. The liquid smoke can be substituted with 1 teaspoon of smoked paprika and 1 teaspoon of soy sauce, but this will alter the color.

1 (14-oz) can white beans, drained and rinsed

1 (14-oz) can whole hearts of palm, drained

¼ cup finely chopped celery

1 tablespoon finely chopped red onion

3 tablespoons vegan mayonnaise

1 teaspoon Dijon mustard

1½ teaspoons liquid smoke

½ teaspoon lemon zest

½ teaspoon dulse flakes

1 teaspoon lemon juice

3 tablespoons minced fresh dill, divided

Salt

Black pepper

INTRODUCING HEARTS OF PALM This up-and-coming ingredient can be found in the canned vegetable section of your local grocery store. Like the name suggests, they are the core of palm plants and are preserved in brine. They have a mild flavor with a crunchy exterior and slightly stringy interior.

WHAT IS MALABI? This creamy pudding, made of milk and rose flavoring, is very popular in the Middle East. Traditionally, malabi uses rice flour or semolina as a thickener and is topped with chopped pistachios and raspberry syrup. In some Sephardic homes, malabi is enjoyed during break-fast following Yom Kippur, at Shavuot (where it is customary to eat dairy-rich foods), and at weddings, where it signifies a sweet start to a marriage. Porridges are common in Jewish cuisine, with dishes like mamaliga (Romanian cornmeal porridge), disa (Semolina porridge), and halim (a Persian porridge made of rice, chickpeas, and wheat berries). Many porridge dishes originated during times of hardship, when stretching ingredients was a necessity.

Malabi Porridge with Rose Essence, Pomegranate and Pistachio

SERVES
4

ON THE TABLE IN...
50 minutes

Malabi, an Israeli pudding made of milk, rose essence, sugar, and either rice flour or semolina, was introduced to me as a child by my cousin Yossi, while visiting him in Tel Aviv. Inspired by this unique dish, I created my own hearty breakfast-worthy porridge using brown rice and coconut milk. The fragrant rose essence makes this an unusual but appealing morning meal, or even a light dessert.

Rinse the brown rice in a colander under running water for 10 seconds and transfer it to a medium saucepan. Add the almond milk, lemon zest, salt, and cardamom and bring to a boil over medium heat. Lower the heat to a simmer, cover, and cook until the rice is fully cooked, 35 to 40 minutes.

Add the rose essence, ¼ cup of the chopped pistachios, sugar, and coconut milk and stir until combined. Cook until the mixture is creamy, an additional 5 minutes. Add more sugar, to taste. If the porridge gets too thick, add 1 to 2 tablespoons of additional coconut milk, as needed, to achieve the desired consistency.

Serve with pomegranate seeds and the remaining ¼ cup of chopped pistachios.

1 cup brown jasmine rice

2½ cups plain unsweetened almond milk

¼ teaspoon lemon zest

Pinch sea salt

¼ teaspoon ground cardamom

½ teaspoon rose essence

½ cup chopped pistachios, divided

2 tablespoons sugar, plus more as needed

½ cup canned coconut milk, plus more as needed

1 pomegranate, seeded, or ½ cup pomegranate seeds

NOTE: This recipe uses rose essence, but rose water can be used with this simple conversion: 1 teaspoon rose essence = 1 tablespoon rose water (the appropriate amount in this recipe would be ½ tablespoon). Rose essence can be found in the baking section of larger grocery stores, whereas rose water is typically found in a Middle Eastern or Indian supermarket.

VARIATION: Try using orange blossom water or vanilla extract in place of the rose essence. Use raspberries in place of pomegranate.

SUBSTITUTION: This recipe can also be made using white jasmine rice.

Apple and Honey Porridge Bowl

SERVES
4

ON THE TABLE IN...
25 minutes

This porridge bowl is a Rosh Hashanah–inspired breakfast to fuel you before holiday services. Growing up, the pre-services meal in our house was just as important as the celebratory dinner. I tamed my little grumbling stomach by sneaking caramel candies and kosher fruit candies from my dad's tallit (prayer shawl) bag. If you are going to be sitting in synagogue for services, you'll need something hearty and filling, and this porridge will keep your rumbling tummy from allowing you to enjoy the services. It's also a recipe that is full of apples and honey for a sweet start to the New Year celebrations.

APPLE TOPPING

2 medium Granny Smith apples, peeled and thinly sliced

1 tablespoon lemon juice

1 tablespoon coconut oil

2 tablespoons honey

⅓ cup water

1 teaspoon ground cinnamon

1 teaspoon finely chopped fresh ginger

1 teaspoon vanilla extract

PORRIDGE

4 cups plain unsweetened almond milk

¼ teaspoon sea salt

2 cups rolled oats, gluten-free, if preferred

2 teaspoons vanilla extract

2 tablespoons chia seeds

½ cup chopped walnuts

Make the apple topping Place the apple slices in a bowl. Toss them with the lemon juice to prevent browning.

In a nonstick skillet over medium heat, melt the coconut oil. Once hot, add the apples and cook, stirring occasionally, until they begin to soften, 3 to 4 minutes. Add the honey, water, cinnamon, ginger, and vanilla and stir to combine. Cook until the apples have softened, 4 to 5 minutes. Remove from the heat and set aside.

Make the porridge In a medium saucepan, combine the almond milk and salt and bring to a boil over medium heat.

Decrease the heat to low and add the rolled oats. Cook, stirring occasionally, until the oats are soft, about 5 minutes. Remove from the heat and stir in the vanilla and chia seeds.

Spoon the porridge into bowls and top with the cooked apples and chopped walnuts.

NOTE: To prepare in advance, store the cooked oatmeal and apple topping separately. When ready to serve, spoon the oats into a bowl with a splash of almond milk and top with the apples. Microwave in 30-second increments until warmed through.

VARIATION: To make it vegan, omit the honey and use the same amount of agave nectar or maple syrup. Try using pears in place of apples in this recipe.

WHAT IS ROSH HASHANAH? During this celebration of the Jewish New Year, it is traditional to enjoy apples dipped in honey to symbolize that the next twelve months will be sweet. While it is common to associate these two foods with Rosh Hashanah, the holiday has many other symbolic foods, known as *Simanim*, and they include pomegranates, carrots, beets, black-eyed peas, squash, dates, a fish head (I like to use Swedish fish gummies!), and a round challah, signifying continuity.

Lemony Blintzes

SERVES	ON THE TABLE IN…
4 (2 blintzes per serving)	1 hour 20 minutes, including 20 minutes resting time

No Jewish brunch or luncheon is complete without blintzes, the infamous twice-cooked crepes rolled around a creamy cheese filling. Whether fried in butter or baked as a casserole, blintzes are the ultimate break-fast dish. Instead of the more traditional eggy crepe stuffed with a farmer's cheese filling, I modernized the dish by making it vegan, using a mixture of tofu and cashew for the filling and a crepe that uses flax meal in place of eggs.

CREPE BATTER

1½ cups all-purpose flour

2 teaspoons cornstarch

1 tablespoon flax meal

½ teaspoon baking powder

¼ teaspoon sea salt

1 tablespoon maple syrup

1 teaspoon vanilla extract

2 tablespoons neutral oil, such as avocado or grapeseed

2 cups plain unsweetened almond milk

FILLING

1 (14-oz) block extra-firm tofu, drained

¾ cup raw cashews

¼ cup maple syrup

1 teaspoon lemon zest

3 tablespoons lemon juice

1 teaspoon vanilla extract

½ teaspoon almond extract

Pinch sea salt

2 tablespoons coconut oil or vegan butter, divided

Manischewitz Blueberry Compote (page 241) or maple syrup

Make the crepe batter In a large bowl, combine the flour, cornstarch, flax meal, baking powder, salt, maple syrup, vanilla, oil, and almond milk and whisk to blend. Let sit for 20 to 30 minutes. There will be some lumps—it won't get completely smooth.

Make the filling In a food processor or blender, combine the tofu, cashews, maple syrup, lemon zest, lemon juice, vanilla, almond extract, and salt and pulse or blend until smooth.

Cook the crepes Lightly grease a 9-inch nonstick skillet with 1 tablespoon of the coconut oil over medium-low heat. Once melted, wipe the pan using a paper towel and set the oiled paper towel aside to reuse.

Pour a scant ⅓ cup of batter into the pan, immediately swirling the pan to coat the bottom. Cook until the top of the crepe is completely dry, 3 to 4 minutes. Using an offset spatula or silicone spatula, gently flip the crepe and cook on the other side for 1 minute.

Remove the crepe from the pan and place it on a plate or tray. Repeat with the remaining batter, stacking the crepes with a small piece of parchment paper between each one.

Assemble the blintzes Once the crepes have cooled, spoon 2 heaping tablespoons of filling on the bottom third of a crepe, 1 inch from the edge closest to you. Fold in the sides and roll it up tightly. Place the blintz in a baking dish or on a plate with the seam on the bottom. Repeat with the remaining crepes.

Heat the remaining 1 tablespoon of coconut oil in the pan over medium-low heat. Place the blintzes in the pan, seam side down, and cook until golden brown, 3 to 4 minutes per side.

Serve with the compote or syrup.

NOTES: The crepes can be made up to 2 days in advance. Stack them between sheets of wax paper, tightly wrap them in plastic wrap, and store in the fridge. Alternatively, you can roll and assemble the blintzes, wrap them in plastic wrap, and store them in the freezer until needed. To reheat, place them in a baking dish and bake in the oven at 375°F for 12 to 15 minutes, or cook them in a skillet with your choice of butter until heated through (use plant-based butter to make them vegan). To prevent sticking, I find it easiest to wipe out excess oil with a paper towel, and re-wipe the pan between crepes to ensure a very thin coating of oil.

VARIATION: Instead of frying each individual blintz, place them in a buttered 9-by-13-inch baking dish, drizzle with additional melted butter, and bake at 350°F for 30 to 40 minutes, or until golden brown and heated through.

SUBSTITUTION: To save time, try using store-bought crepes (check if vegan) and simply roll them around the filling.

WHAT IS A BLINTZ?

From the Yiddish word *blintze* or the Russian word *blin*, which means "pancake," blintzes are also known in Hungary as *palacsinta*. Compared to crepes, blintzes are generally thicker and simpler to make. Thought to have originated in Slavic countries (largely Poland, Russia, and Ukraine), blintzes are served customarily on Shavuot, when it is common to eat dairy, and after fasting for Yom Kippur.

Halvah Granola

ON THE TABLE IN...
1 hour 10 minutes

My grandparents loved halvah, a sweet confection made with sesame butter and sugar, because it reminded them of their time spent in Israel. Individually wrapped halvah candies could always be found in the depths of their candy drawer. Despite halvah being a sweet confection, sesame seeds are incredibly nutritious and can be a part of healthy breakfast, so it inspired me to toss halvah into my granola in place of dried fruit, for a granola that pays homage to my grandparents' candy drawer and tastes a whole lot better than the raisin-filled granola of my childhood.

3 cups rolled oats, gluten-free, if preferred

½ cup shredded unsweetened coconut

¼ cup chia seeds

¼ cup sesame seeds

⅔ cup pistachios

⅔ cup raw cashews

⅓ cup maple syrup, honey, or agave syrup

¼ cup extra-virgin olive oil

3 tablespoons tahini

2 teaspoons vanilla extract

1 teaspoon ground cinnamon

¼ teaspoon ground cardamom

Pinch sea salt

¾ cup crumbled halvah

Preheat the oven to 275°F. Line a large sheet pan with parchment paper and set aside.

In a large bowl, combine the oats, coconut, chia seeds, sesame seeds, pistachios, and cashews.

In a medium bowl, whisk together the maple syrup, olive oil, tahini, vanilla, cinnamon, cardamom, and salt. Add the wet mixture to the dry mixture and stir until combined.

Transfer the mixture to the prepared sheet pan and spread it out in an even layer. Bake for 1 hour, stirring every 20 minutes. Remove from the oven and sprinkle with the halvah. Let cool on the sheet pan.

Transfer the granola to an airtight container and store at room temperature for up to 10 days.

NOTE: If you want to add dried fruit to your granola, toss it in as soon as the sheet pan is removed from the oven. The heat from the granola will soften the dried fruit and help it stick to the pieces. Don't bake the dried fruit with the nuts and seeds, though, because the high sugar content of dried fruits will cause them to burn.

VARIATION: Add an egg white to the liquid ingredients in your granola to make it even crunchier with larger clusters. Egg whites act as a binder, and the addition can help the components stick together. Love cardamom? Add an extra ¼ teaspoon!

WHAT IS MATZO FARFEL?

This recipe uses whole sheets of matzo, broken into small pieces, in lieu of matzo farfel, which is simply matzo broken into smaller pieces and comes packaged as a Passover product that you may feel compelled to buy. Instead, buy whole sheets of matzo, break up whatever you need for Passover, and use the rest in whatever way you please for the rest of the year.

Matzo Olive Oil Granola

SERVES
6 to 8

ON THE TABLE IN...
1 hour 10 minutes

I have less-than-fond memories of boxed cereal during Passover, where the flavorless (and expensive) cereal would disintegrate in my milk, leave me hungry five minutes later, and make me count the seconds until Passover was over. For me, Passover breakfast poses the most challenges—there's no toast, oats, bagels, or pancakes (besides my Passover-Friendly All-Year Pancakes, page 64) and very few on-the-go options that you can transport to work, travel with, or nosh on during the day. That's why I've added matzo granola to my Passover menus. Hint: Add dried fruit to granola right after taking it out of the oven! My favorite part about this recipe? It is entirely customizable to your preferences, pantry, and family!

Preheat the oven to 300°F. Line a large sheet pan with parchment paper.

In a large bowl, break the matzo into small pieces. Add the almonds, cashews, walnuts, coconut, chia seeds, and flax seeds and stir to combine.

In a small bowl, whisk together the maple syrup, olive oil, cinnamon, ginger, and salt. Pour the wet mixture into the dry mixture and stir to combine.

Transfer the mixture to the prepared sheet pan and spread in an even layer. Bake for 1 hour, stirring every 20 minutes, or until golden.

Immediately after removing from the oven, add the dried fruit, stirring to evenly distribute. Let cool before transferring to jars or containers.

3 sheets of matzo or 2 cups matzo farfel

1 cup almonds, roughly chopped

½ cup cashews, roughly chopped

½ cup walnuts, roughly chopped

½ cup shredded unsweetened coconut

3 tablespoons chia seeds

3 tablespoons flax seeds

¼ cup maple syrup

¼ cup extra-virgin olive oil

1 teaspoon ground cinnamon

½ teaspoon ground ginger

¼ teaspoon sea salt

½ cup chopped dried fruits (any type)

NOTE: Store the granola in an airtight container at room temperature for up to 1 week, in the fridge for up to 2 weeks, or in the freezer for up to 3 months.

VARIATION: Change this granola to suit your own Passover preferences. If you eat seeds, add ½ cup sesame seeds, sunflower seeds, or pumpkin seeds in place of the nuts. Can't stand raisins? Go ahead and leave them out. Want it chocolatey? Add ½ cup chocolate chips right after you take the granola out of the oven. Love clumpy granola? Add an egg white with the liquid ingredients.

Passover-Friendly All-Year Pancakes

SERVES
4 (makes 10 to 12 pancakes)

ON THE TABLE IN...
30 minutes

Gone are the days when Passover breakfast meant flavorless cereals or matzo with cream cheese. With the availability of alternative flours, such as almond, coconut, and chickpea (if Sephardic), Passover baking has never been better, and these pancakes are no exception. They are great for the holiday and beyond, and there's no reason to settle at breakfast time during the holidays. I love topping my pancakes with Greek or coconut yogurt, nut butters, and fresh fruit, but get creative with your toppings!

1½ cups almond flour, sifted

1 tablespoon baking powder, kosher for Passover

¼ teaspoon ground cinnamon

¼ teaspoon sea salt

½ cup plain unsweetened almond milk

1 tablespoon honey or maple syrup

1 tablespoon vanilla extract, kosher for Passover, if required, or omit

2 large eggs

2 large egg whites, at room temperature

Butter or oil, for cooking

SUBSTITUTION:
If you can't find kosher-for-Passover baking powder, use an additional egg white and whip until soft peaks form, then gently fold the egg whites into the almond flour mixture, as instructed.

Preheat the oven to 200°F. Line a sheet pan with parchment paper. Set aside.

In a large bowl, sift together the almond flour, baking powder, cinnamon, and salt.

In a liquid measuring cup or small bowl, whisk together the milk, honey, vanilla (if using), and whole eggs. Add to the almond flour mixture and stir with a silicone spatula until just combined.

In a medium bowl, whisk the egg whites until white, opaque, and foamy, about 3 minutes.

Fold half the egg whites into the almond flour mixture, using a rubber spatula to gently combine, then add the remaining egg whites and gently combine. Note: Do not do this in advance, otherwise the egg whites will lose their volume.

Heat a nonstick skillet over medium-low heat. Lightly grease with butter or oil. Using a ¼-cup measure, scoop the batter into the pan, about 3 pancakes at a time. Let cook until the top begins to bubble and is no longer shiny, 4 to 5 minutes. Carefully flip and cook until browned on the other side, 1 to 2 minutes. Transfer to the prepared sheet pan and keep warm in the oven while repeating with the remaining batter.

NOTE: When whipping egg whites, if there is the presence of any fat, they will not whip correctly, so make sure the bowl is super clean before adding the eggs. I like to rinse mine with a splash of vinegar just to be sure. Room-temperature egg whites will whip higher than fresh from the fridge, due to an increased surface area.

Almond Flour Crepes

SERVES
4 (2 crepes per serving)

ON THE TABLE IN...
45 minutes

As a kid, I thought that Passover was an incredible challenge. A week without bread, bagels, or cereal? Unimaginable. With time, I've come to see it as a way to get creative in the kitchen and try new foods. The rise of "grain-free" and "paleo" diets created space to experiment with recipes like never before. This grain-free crepe recipe is not only Passover-friendly, but it's also a great way to enjoy crepes all year-round, fitting into both gluten-free and low-carb diets. Packed with heart-healthy fats and protein, almond flour is the secret ingredient in your Passover kitchen.

In a medium bowl, whisk the eggs, sugar, almond flour, and cinnamon until well combined and no lumps remain. Set aside.

Heat the butter in a 9-inch nonstick skillet over medium-low heat. Once melted, wipe the pan using a paper towel and set the buttered paper towel aside to reuse. Pour a scant ⅓ cup of batter into the pan, immediately swirling the pan to evenly coat the bottom. Cook until the top is dry, 2 to 3 minutes. Using a silicone spatula, loosen the sides, carefully flip the crepe, and cook the other side until dry, 1 to 2 minutes.

Place the crepe on a plate and repeat with the remaining batter, wiping the pan with the buttered paper towel in between each crepe and stacking the crepes between sheets of parchment paper or wax paper as you go.

Fill each crepe with whipped cream, charoset, nut butter, or berries and serve.

8 large eggs

2 tablespoons sugar

⅔ cup almond flour, sifted

1 teaspoon ground cinnamon

1 tablespoon butter or coconut oil, for cooking

Whipped cream, charoset, nut butter, or berries, for serving

NOTE: Unfilled crepes can be placed between sheets of wax paper, tightly wrapped in plastic wrap, and stored in the fridge for up to 3 days or in the freezer for up to 3 months. To reheat, place them in a skillet over medium-low heat until warmed through.

VARIATIONS: Make these into Passover-friendly blintzes by rolling them with your favorite blintz filling, or my vegan filling (Lemony Blintzes, page 56). Want a savory crepe? Omit the sugar and cinnamon and add ¼ teaspoon sea salt. Serve filled with eggs, grated cheese, and/or avocado. Add 2 teaspoons of vanilla extract if making outside of Passover.

DIY ALMOND FLOUR Make your own almond flour by pulsing almonds in the food processor or blender until it turns into a fine meal. Sift well. Note that using almonds with skin will result in a darker flour.

Soups

Chickpea Noodle Vegetable Soup

SERVES	ON THE TABLE IN...		
6	1 hour		

There's a common belief that chicken soup is Jewish penicillin—and most ailments can be fixed with a bowl of steaming soup from any bubbe's kitchen. While my days of chicken soup may be behind me as I've transitioned to a plant-based diet, I still crave the comfort that it provides. Instead of chicken, I turn to this chickpea soup in its place for a savory hug in a bowl. Seasoned with miso paste, lemon zest, and dill, this savory soup is equally as comforting and hearty. In Ashkenazi custom, parsnips are added for a sweet, earthy flavor. Replacing the chicken with chickpeas keeps a source of protein, and hearty noodles make this a meal-worthy soup.

2 tablespoons extra-virgin olive oil

1 medium white or yellow onion, chopped

1 large parsnip, sliced into ¼-inch rounds

4 medium carrots, sliced into ¼-inch rounds

4 stalks celery, chopped into ¼-inch pieces

1 medium fennel bulb, cored and chopped into ¼-inch pieces

3 garlic cloves, finely chopped

1 sprig fresh thyme

10 cups vegetable broth, low-sodium if preferred

1 (14-oz) can chickpeas, drained and rinsed

1 teaspoon lemon zest

Juice of 1 lemon

4 ounces egg noodles, gluten-free or vegan, if preferred

1 tablespoon yellow or white miso paste

½ teaspoon black pepper

½ teaspoon sea salt

¼ cup chopped fresh dill

Heat the olive oil in a large pot over medium heat until hot. Add the onion, parsnip, carrots, celery, fennel, and garlic, stirring to combine. Cook for 8 to 10 minutes, or until the vegetables begin to soften.

Add the thyme, vegetable broth, chickpeas, lemon zest, and lemon juice and bring to a boil. Lower the heat and simmer for 20 to 25 minutes.

Bring the liquid back to a boil, add the egg noodles, and cook until al dente, 4 to 5 minutes.

Remove from the heat and stir in the miso. Taste, and season with salt and pepper. Serve with fresh dill.

NOTE: To avoid soggy noodles, add them just before serving. If you're making the soup in advance and plan to freeze it, do not add the noodles. To reheat, bring the soup to a boil, add the noodles, and cook them in the soup for 4 to 5 minutes right before serving.

VARIATIONS: To make this kosher for Passover, omit the noodles. If you eat beans during Passover, keep the chickpeas and miso in the soup. If you don't eat beans, omit the chickpeas and miso and double the vegetables for a heartier soup. You may need to reduce the vegetable broth used. I love using a can of light beer in soups, as it imparts a slightly bitter depth of flavor. After cooking, the alcohol evaporates and you are left with a funky, but pleasing, rich flavor.

WHAT IS MISO?

Miso is a fermented paste made with a combination of beans (typically soybeans), grains, salt, and koji, a type of (edible!) mold. Miso originated in Japan, where miso-making is a true art form. It has a similar consistency to peanut butter and gives a salty, savory flavor to any dish it is added to. Miso is a staple ingredient in many plant-based kitchens for building rich flavor, without meat!

WHAT IS BORSCHT? Beet borscht is synonymous with Russian, Polish, and Ukrainian cuisine. The term *borscht* generally refers to sour-tasting soups, whether made with or without beets. It was the Ukrainian version with its distinctive red color that became widely popular in North America and is what we commonly refer to as borscht today. With its evolution, the use of potatoes, beet greens, and sour cream has varied across the Diaspora and cultures. Given that many enjoy serving it with sour cream, vegetarian versions are common, to avoid combining meat and dairy. Borscht can be served either hot or cold with buttermilk or sour cream.

Fennel and Beet Borscht

SERVES
8

ON THE TABLE IN...
1 hour

Although my great-grandmother emigrated from Ukraine to Canada as a young woman, her love for her country's traditional cuisine never faltered. She brought with her the recipes of her childhood, sharing them among the generations that followed. In Canada, winters are long, meaning root vegetables are seemingly always in season, and they find their way into many dishes. Unsurprisingly, beet borscht was a staple dish in our family. This vegan version is an ode to my family's borscht, updated with fresh fennel, savory miso, and a creamy coconut milk garnish.

In a large pot, heat the olive oil over medium heat. Add the onion and cook, stirring occasionally, until it begins to soften, 6 to 8 minutes.

Add the fennel, carrots, garlic, and potatoes and cook until the vegetables begin to soften slightly, an additional 5 to 6 minutes.

Add the grated beets, chopped cabbage, broth, bay leaf, salt, and pepper. Bring the mixture to a boil, decrease the heat to low, and simmer for 15 to 20 minutes.

Add the lemon zest, lemon juice, miso, and dill, and stir to combine. Season with salt and pepper to taste.

Serve in bowls, drizzled with about 1 tablespoon of coconut milk per bowl and sprinkled with additional dill.

NOTES: Peeling beets is a messy job—be sure to wear an apron, dark clothing, and gloves (I know I always do!). Store in an airtight container in the fridge for up to 4 days or freeze for up to 6 months. To make this Passover-friendly, omit the miso.

VARIATIONS: Substitute dairy kefir for the coconut milk, if preferred. Add a 14-oz can of drained and rinsed white beans to this dish for additional protein.

- 2 tablespoons extra-virgin olive oil
- 1 medium yellow onion, cut into ½-inch pieces
- 2 fennel bulbs, quartered, cored, and roughly chopped
- 2 medium carrots, sliced into ¼-inch rounds
- 2 garlic cloves, finely chopped
- 1 pound baby potatoes, quartered
- 2 large beets, peeled and grated
- ½ medium green cabbage, finely chopped
- 6 cups vegetable broth, low-sodium if preferred
- 1 bay leaf
- ½ teaspoon sea salt, plus more as needed
- ¼ teaspoon black pepper, plus more as needed
- 1 teaspoon lemon zest
- 2 tablespoons lemon juice
- 1 tablespoon white or yellow miso paste
- ½ cup chopped fresh dill, plus more for serving
- ½ cup canned coconut milk, for serving

Sweet and Sour Cabbage Soup

ON THE TABLE IN...
1 hour

This is traditionally made using a tough cut of beef and simmered low and slow, resulting in a rich soup sweetened with lemon juice and sugar. Cabbage soup was one of my favorites growing up, and I used to pick out the pieces of meat, focusing on the cabbage and chunky tomatoes instead. My grandmother would be so upset by this act of defiance. Yet, to this day, when visiting a specific deli (Sherman's, in Palm Springs, California) I order the cabbage soup and pick out the meat. Old habits die hard! This recipe uses both maple syrup and sweet potatoes for sweetness, which is cut by the acidic tomatoes and apple cider vinegar for a lovely balance of flavors. I also like to add sauerkraut to the soup for a savory twist on the classic.

2 tablespoons extra-virgin olive oil

1 medium yellow onion, finely chopped

2 garlic cloves, finely chopped

2 tablespoons tomato paste

2 tablespoons sweet paprika

1 medium (about 2-lb) head green cabbage, quartered and thinly sliced

3 medium carrots, cut into ½-inch pieces

1 sweet potato, peeled and cut into ½-inch pieces

1 bay leaf

8 cups vegetable broth, low-sodium if preferred

1 (28-oz) can crushed tomatoes

¼ cup apple cider vinegar

3 tablespoons maple syrup, plus more as needed

2 tablespoons lemon juice

¾ cup sauerkraut

Salt

Black pepper

¼ cup chopped fresh parsley, for serving

Heat the oil in a 4- or 5-quart heavy-bottomed pot over medium heat. Add the onion, garlic, tomato paste, and paprika and cook until the onion begins to soften slightly, 3 to 4 minutes.

Add the cabbage, carrots, sweet potato, and bay leaf to the pot. Pour the broth, crushed tomatoes, vinegar, and maple syrup over the cabbage and stir to combine. Bring to a boil over medium-high heat and simmer, stirring occasionally, until the cabbage is fully cooked and tender, 25 to 30 minutes.

Add the lemon juice and sauerkraut and simmer over low heat for an additional 5 minutes. Remove the bay leaf and discard. Season with salt and pepper to taste. Add more maple syrup as needed.

Serve topped with fresh parsley and freshly ground pepper.

NOTE: Store the soup in airtight containers in the fridge for up to 4 days or in the freezer for up to 6 months. If freezing, portion it into 2- or 4-serving containers so you aren't stuck eating the same soup every day for a week!

VARIATION: Make this soup into an even heartier meal by adding 2 (14-oz) cans of drained and rinsed white beans.

WHICH CABBAGE IS BEST?

Cabbage is the base for this delicious soup. When you add the cabbage to the pot, it will be voluminous, but as it cooks, it will lose volume, fitting perfectly and releasing its flavor into the broth. For this recipe, use green cabbage for best results. Red or purple cabbage will change the color of the soup (though the flavor will be fine), whereas napa or savoy cabbage will change the texture of the soup. In a pinch, you can substitute bagged, preshredded cabbage to save on prep time.

A LITTLE ABOUT LENTILS Lentils are a great way to introduce plant-based protein to your recipes. Unlike other beans or legumes, they do not require overnight soaking and cook relatively quickly. There are four main categories of lentils: brown, green, red, and specialty (like beluga). Brown lentils are the most common variety and have a mild taste. They hold their shape when cooked and can be found dried or canned, ready to toss on top of salads. Green lentils take longer to cook and are the firmest variety when cooked. This recipe uses red lentils, which are nutty in taste. Red lentils are sold "split," meaning they are quick to cook and lose their shape when cooking, which helps thicken this soup. Once cooked, they become golden yellow in color.

Yossi's Lemony Lentil Soup

SERVES	ON THE TABLE IN...	
6	55 minutes	

My cousin Yossi was born and raised in Israel. Every time we saw him, he would share his passion for Israeli cuisine with our family. If there is one meal he was guaranteed to serve, it would be cumin-scented lemon lentil soup with fresh homemade pita. Inspired by his recipe, I created this variation, which has become my go-to weeknight soup. The red lentils make for quick cooking and an easy, freezer-friendly one-pot meal. My take on this dish is packed with lemon zest and juice, for a zippy soup that is guaranteed to warm you from the inside out. It has long been my husband's favorite dish!

Heat the olive oil in a large pot over medium heat. Add the onion and cook until it begins to soften, 5 to 6 minutes.

Add the garlic, lentils, rice, cumin, and coriander, stirring to evenly coat with the spices. Stir in the salt and pepper. Pour in the vegetable stock and bring to a boil. Decrease the heat to medium-low, cover, and simmer for an additional 22 to 25 minutes, or until the lentils are yellow and broken down.

Add the lemon zest and juice. Use an immersion or hand blender to puree the soup until smooth or transfer the soup to a blender and puree. Season with salt and pepper to taste.

Serve garnished with chopped parsley.

2 tablespoons extra-virgin olive oil

1 medium yellow onion, finely chopped

8 garlic cloves, finely chopped

1 cup dried red lentils, rinsed

½ cup jasmine rice, rinsed

1 tablespoon ground cumin

1 teaspoon ground coriander

¼ teaspoon sea salt, plus more as needed

¼ teaspoon black pepper, plus more as needed

8 cups vegetable stock

Zest of 2 lemons

Juice of 3 lemons (about ⅓ cup)

⅓ cup chopped fresh parsley, for garnish

NOTE: Leftover soup keeps well in an airtight container in the fridge for up to 4 days and can be reheated in a microwave or on the stove. Freeze leftovers for up to 3 months. Let it thaw in the fridge overnight before reheating.

VARIATION: Skip the blending for a chunkier version of this soup. I love this soup extra lemony. If you prefer less lemon juice, start with ¼ cup and add more to taste.

Poppy Seed, Potato, and Caramelized Onion Kreplach

MAKES
About 3 dozen

ON THE TABLE IN...
2 hours 30 minutes, including
15 minutes resting time

Kreplach are Eastern European soup dumplings, filled with anything from leftover meat to potatoes. They are often served in a savory broth or with fried onions. My grandmother Eva was known for her kreplach. She filled them with her famed roast chicken or potatoes and lovingly folded them into neat, triangular pockets. One of my favorite memories of her was when I introduced her to my (now) husband and we folded dozens upon dozens of kreplach to float in our Shabbat soup. With a flavorful filling and soft dough, and studded with poppy seeds, this vegan variation on the classic is my go-to, and I often serve it in my Turmeric Vegetable Matzo Ball Soup (page 83).

FILLING
1 tablespoon olive oil
2 medium yellow onions, finely chopped
2 garlic cloves, peeled
2 medium or 1 large Yukon gold potatoes, peeled and quartered
¼ teaspoon sea salt
¼ teaspoon black pepper

DOUGH
2 cups all-purpose flour
1 tablespoon cornstarch
½ teaspoon sea salt
½ to ¾ cup water
2 tablespoons olive oil
1½ teaspoons poppy seeds

TO ASSEMBLE
1 tablespoon cornstarch
¼ cup water

Make the filling Heat the olive oil in a medium skillet over medium-low heat. Add the onions and cook, stirring occasionally, until golden, 25 to 30 minutes.

Decrease the heat to low, add the garlic, and cook for an additional 10 to 15 minutes. The onions should be a deep golden brown and reduced in size.

While the onions are cooking, in a medium saucepan, combine the potatoes with enough water to cover and bring to a boil over medium heat. Boil until the potatoes are fork-tender, 10 to 15 minutes. Drain the potatoes and mash them with a fork or potato masher.

Add the onion and garlic mixture, salt, and pepper to the mashed potatoes and mix until well combined. The saltiness of the filling will be muted by the dough, so it should taste well-seasoned.

Make the dough Combine the flour, cornstarch, salt, ½ cup of water, and olive oil in a bowl or food processor and mix or process until a dough forms. Add more water, 1 tablespoon at a time, as needed, for the dough to form into a smooth and soft ball.

continued

Add the poppy seeds and mix or pulse a few times to distribute them evenly. When you roll out the dough, it will distribute the poppy seeds as well. Form the dough into a disk, cover with plastic wrap, and refrigerate for at least 15 minutes or up to overnight.

Assemble the kreplach Combine the cornstarch and water in a small bowl.

On a lightly floured surface, roll the dough into a rectangle $\frac{1}{16}$ to $\frac{1}{8}$ inch thick. It should be slightly thinner than a pierogi, but thicker than a wonton. Using a small knife, cut the dough into 3-by-3-inch squares.

Dip your finger into the cornstarch mixture and run it around the edges of each square as you go. Doing this to every piece of dough ahead of time will result in soggy dough and will be hard to shape. Place 1 teaspoon of potato and onion filling in the middle of the square. Fold the dough into a triangle enveloping the filling, then pinch the edges to seal. Take the bottom corners and press to join. Set aside and repeat with the rest of the dough and filling.

Bring a large pot of water to a boil over high heat. Add the kreplach and cook in the boiling water until they float to the surface, 3 to 4 minutes.

Serve the kreplach in a bowl of soup or fry them in a skillet with sliced onions.

NOTE: Kreplach can be made in advance. Once stuffed and sealed, place the kreplach on a lightly floured sheet pan and place in the freezer for at least 4 hours, or until the kreplach are solid. Transfer the kreplach to a zip-top freezer bag and freeze for up to 3 months. To serve, cook them in boiling water straight from the freezer and add to your soup, or fry them with onions.

VARIATIONS: Kreplach can be filled with almost anything! Try leftover mashed sweet potatoes, tofu ricotta, or even mashed chickpeas.

EASIER KREPLACH
Making your own dough is simple, but it can be time-consuming. Feel free to use premade dumpling or wonton wrappers. You can find them in many Asian grocery stores or in the refrigerated aisle of the grocery store, often near the tofu and plant-based protein alternatives.

ALL ABOUT MATZO BALLS
We don't know exactly how matzo balls (Yiddish: *kneidlach* or German: *knodel*) came to be. Some believe that Jews would repurpose matzo crumbs and add them to soup for a more filling meal, while some believe that it was a means of utilizing an overproduction of matzo meal. Regardless, it wasn't until Manischewitz packaged up ground matzo meal stateside and marketed it as a dumpling mix that we started calling it a matzo ball in 1902.

Turmeric Vegetable Matzo Ball Soup

SERVES
6

ON THE TABLE IN...
1 hour

If chicken soup is Jewish penicillin, then matzo ball soup is the key to world peace. Matzo balls are synonymous with comfort, family, and, of course, Passover. My favorite thing to eat during Passover was a matzo ball... no soup, no garnish, simply a matzo ball. Whenever I go to a Jewish deli, no matter what I order, I order a matzo ball as a side. This golden soup is my modern take on my grandmother's famed chicken soup. Seasoned with ginger, turmeric, and a pinch of red chili flakes, it is a warming soup that is full of nutritious ingredients and is a soup for the soul!

In a large pot, heat the olive oil over medium heat. Add the onion and cook until it begins to soften, 5 to 6 minutes. Add the carrots, celery, and garlic and cook until they begin to soften, 4 to 5 minutes.

Add the ginger, turmeric, cumin, paprika, salt, pepper, and chili flakes and stir until combined. Pour in 9 cups of the vegetable broth and bring to a boil. Decrease the heat and simmer, partially covered, for 25 minutes.

Remove from the heat. Taste the soup; if it is too salty or spicy, add the remaining 1 cup of vegetable broth, as needed. Add the lemon juice and mix well. Season with salt and pepper to taste.

Serve with chopped cilantro and matzo balls.

> **NOTE:** Freeze the soup in airtight containers for up to 6 months.
>
> **VARIATION:** If making this soup outside of Passover, add a 12-oz can of light beer or cider in place of some of the broth for a richer flavor.

1 tablespoon extra-virgin olive oil

1 medium white onion, cut into ½-inch pieces

5 medium carrots, cut into ¼-inch slices

3 stalks celery, cut into ½-inch pieces

4 garlic cloves, finely chopped

1 tablespoon freshly grated ginger

1 teaspoon ground turmeric

½ teaspoon ground cumin

½ teaspoon sweet paprika

½ teaspoon sea salt, plus more as needed

¼ teaspoon black pepper, plus more as needed

¼ teaspoon red chili flakes

9 to 10 cups vegetable broth, low-sodium if preferred

Juice of 1 lemon

½ cup chopped fresh cilantro

Vegan Matzo Balls (page 84)

Vegan Matzo Balls

MAKES
10 to 12 matzo balls

ON THE TABLE IN...
6 hours, including at least
4 hours 15 minutes resting time

If you thought eating foods that are traditionally made with eggs was off the table, think again! These matzo balls are made with ground flax, baking powder, chickpea liquid (aquafaba), and chickpea flour to replace the fat, lift, and binding properties of eggs. Inspired by gondi, a Persian chickpea dumpling soup, this recipe for vegan matzo balls is anything but ordinary. While not suitable for those who avoid kitniyot during Passover, these matzo balls can be enjoyed year-round.

1 cup matzo meal

2 tablespoons chickpea flour

1 tablespoon ground flax seeds

1 tablespoon baking powder,
   kosher for Passover

1 teaspoon salt

1 teaspoon garlic powder

½ teaspoon black pepper

½ teaspoon onion powder

¼ cup extra-virgin olive oil

½ cup liquid from canned
   chickpeas or white beans
   (aquafaba)

⅓ cup seltzer water

3 tablespoons chopped fresh dill

NOTE: To reheat vegan matzo balls, add them to a greased steamer basket and steam until warmed through, 15 to 20 minutes.

In a medium bowl, whisk together the matzo meal, chickpea flour, flax seeds, baking powder, salt, garlic powder, black pepper, and onion powder. Add the olive oil, aquafaba, seltzer, and dill and stir until just combined. Cover with plastic wrap and refrigerate for at least 4 hours, or up to overnight.

When ready to cook, firmly roll 1 heaping tablespoon of the mixture into a ball, approximately the size of a golf ball, and place on a plate. Repeat with the rest of the mixture. Cover with plastic wrap and return to the fridge for 15 minutes.

Generously grease a steamer basket with oil. Set the steamer basket fitted with a lid in a large pot of water, ensuring that the water does not touch the bottom of the steamer basket. Place over medium-high heat, and bring to a boil. Once the water is boiling, decrease the heat to medium-low and add the matzo balls to the basket. Note: They will not expand very much, so they can be placed close to one another. Cover with the lid and steam for 25 minutes. Carefully remove the matzo balls from the steamer basket using a spatula.

Add the matzo balls to soup when ready to eat.

FIXING SALTY SOUP There is a fine line between well-seasoned soup and salty soup. If you find that your soup is too salty, try one of these tips:
- Add 1 cup of water or low-sodium broth.
- Add a halved potato. Simmer for 20 to 30 minutes, and then remove the potato before serving; the potato will soak up excess salt.
- Add a squeeze of lemon juice or vinegar to counteract the saltiness.

Floater Herbed Matzo Balls

MAKES
15 to 18 matzo balls

ON THE TABLE IN...
1 hour 30 minutes,
including 35 minutes resting time

In my household, matzo balls always came from a mix, and it wasn't until recently that I thought outside the box by replacing the salty mix with fresh herbs and spices. I like to use rich olive oil in place of chicken schmaltz in my matzo balls, because it gives a depth of flavor that vegetable oil can't, not to mention a beautiful golden hue.

In a medium bowl, whisk together the matzo meal, baking powder, salt, garlic powder, and onion powder. Add the whisked eggs, olive oil, soda water, chives, dill, parsley, and lemon zest and mix until just combined. Cover with plastic wrap and refrigerate for 20 minutes.

When ready to cook, roll 1 heaping tablespoon of the mixture into a ball, approximately the size of a golf ball, and place on a plate. Repeat with the rest of the mixture. Cover with plastic wrap and refrigerate for 15 minutes while you prepare the cooking water.

Bring a large pot of water or vegetable broth to a boil over high heat. Once boiling, decrease the heat to medium-low and add the matzo balls. Cover with a lid and simmer until they are fluffy and fully cooked, 30 to 40 minutes. Do not lift the lid to peek before 30 minutes.

Serve in your favorite soup, like Turmeric Vegetable Matzo Ball Soup (page 83).

NOTE: Matzo balls can be frozen! Let them come to room temperature. Line a sheet pan with parchment paper, place the matzo balls on the pan, and freeze for 2 to 3 hours, or until firm. Transfer the matzo balls to a freezer bag and freeze. Matzo balls can be reheated directly in your soup.

VARIATION: Add your favorite herbs to the matzo ball recipes. I use a mixture of parsley, dill, and chives, but get creative and use tarragon, cilantro, or even basil.

1 cup matzo meal

1 teaspoon baking powder

1 teaspoon salt

½ teaspoon garlic powder

½ teaspoon onion powder

4 large eggs, whisked

¼ cup extra-virgin olive oil

¼ cup soda water or seltzer

1 tablespoon chopped fresh chives

1 tablespoon finely chopped fresh dill

2 tablespoons finely chopped fresh parsley

½ teaspoon lemon zest

10 to 12 cups water or vegetable broth, for cooking

TIPS FOR FLOATER MATZO BALLS

I am a firm proponent of floaters, so here are things you can do to avoid sinkers:

- Add baking powder to your matzo balls.
- Use soda water.
- Don't overwork the mixture when rolling into balls.
- Separate the eggs and whip the whites until foamy.

Salads, Spreads & Sides

Everything Bagel "Fattoush" Salad with Za'atar Cheeseballs

SERVES	ON THE TABLE IN…	
6	25 minutes	

There's a misconception that salads are boring, lifeless, and sad bowls of green lettuce. It doesn't have to be that way. This lettuce-free salad is inspired by the tomato and cucumber salads served in Israeli cuisine, but it is in a league of its own, with crunchy bagel croutons (hint: let them sit in the dressing to soften slightly, and use them to scoop the salad!), and creamy bite-size za'atar-spiced cheeseballs made with soft vegan cheese or goat cheese. It is a crave-worthy salad that is anything but ordinary.

CROUTONS
1 bagel, cut into ¼-inch slices

1½ tablespoon extra-virgin olive oil

1 tablespoon Everything Bagel Spice (page 246) or store-bought

CHEESEBALLS
½ cup goat cheese or soft vegan cheese, if preferred

2 tablespoons za'atar

SALAD
1 large English cucumber, diced

1 pint cherry tomatoes, quartered

½ medium yellow onion, finely chopped

2 cups chopped fresh parsley

1½ teaspoons lemon zest

Juice of 2 lemons

3 tablespoons extra-virgin olive oil

¼ teaspoon sea salt

¼ teaspoon black pepper

Make the croutons Preheat the oven to 350°F. Line a sheet pan with parchment paper.

In a medium bowl, toss the bagel slices, olive oil, and everything bagel spice until combined. Transfer the slices to the prepared sheet pan and toast for 10 minutes.

Make the cheeseballs While the bagel slices are toasting, use a ½-teaspoon measure to scoop the soft cheese into balls. Place the za'atar in a shallow dish. Roll the balls of cheese in the za'atar to coat. Set aside.

Make the salad In a serving bowl, combine the cucumber, cherry tomatoes, onion, parsley, lemon zest, lemon juice, and olive oil. Season with salt and pepper.

Top the salad with the bagel croutons and cheese balls. Serve immediately.

NOTES: To prepare in advance, combine the vegetables and dressing and store in an airtight container in the refrigerator. Before serving, toss the dressed vegetables with the croutons and cheeseballs. The cheeseballs can be made up to 1 week in advance and refrigerated in an airtight container. Store the croutons in an airtight container at room temperature for up to 3 days.

VARIATION: During Passover, omit the bagel croutons and substitute toasted matzo dressed with olive oil and garlic powder for an equally delicious salad.

ISRAELI VS. FATTOUSH SALAD

Fattoush is a salad made with toasted or fried flatbread, mixed greens, tomatoes, cucumbers, and radishes, whereas Israeli salad is a chopped salad of tomatoes, onions, cucumber, and peppers and is served alongside everything from breakfast to dinner. While outside of Israel we refer to this salad as "Israeli salad," within Israel it is simply called "chopped salad."

WHY DO WE EAT HORSERADISH ON PASSOVER?

Horseradish symbolizes the bitterness that the Jewish people experienced as slaves in Egypt. It is a means of symbolic "suffering" in remembrance of the Passover story and is one of the seven symbolic foods on the seder plate.

Herbed Horseradish Salad

SERVES
6

ON THE TABLE IN...
25 minutes

We have a tradition in my house during the seder that when we are instructed to "point to the bitter herb [horseradish]" we point to my mom. The story was that when she was younger and a grumpy guest at the family seder table, when it came to point to the bitter herb, her family pointed to her, paving the way for her nickname, Herb. This salad is a vibrant side for Passover or at any time of the year, with fresh herbs, tangy dressing, and an addictive almond crunch topping.

Make the almond crunch In a small saucepan over medium heat, combine the olive oil, almond flakes, fennel seeds, sliced garlic, and sunflower seeds and cook until the almonds and garlic begin to brown, 4 to 5 minutes. The garlic should be crisp. Remove from the heat, add the salt, and mix well.

Transfer the mixture to a heatproof dish and let cool to room temperature. Transfer to an airtight jar or container and store in a cool, dark place for up to 3 days.

Make the dressing In a small bowl, whisk together the lemon zest, lemon juice, horseradish, and maple syrup. Slowly drizzle in the olive oil and whisk until combined. Season with salt and pepper to taste.

Make the salad Combine the butter lettuce, fennel, radicchio, cucumber, parsley, dill, basil, and chives in a large bowl.

Toss with the dressing and the almond crumble before serving.

> **NOTE:** This recipe is a great way to use up leftover herbs. Feel free to substitute any fresh, leafy herbs you have on hand, like mint, tarragon, or cilantro.
>
> **VARIATION:** The magic in this recipe lies in the almond crunch topping, which is a Passover-friendly crouton alternative. Substitute your favorite chopped nuts for the almonds, add a thinly sliced shallot, or add a chopped chili pepper for a little extra heat. If you don't eat kitniyot during Passover, omit the fennel seeds and sunflower seeds and replace them with additional Passover-friendly nuts like cashews or pistachios.

ALMOND CRUNCH TOPPING
¼ cup extra-virgin olive oil

½ cup almond flakes

2 tablespoons fennel seeds

4 garlic cloves, thinly sliced

1 tablespoon sunflower seeds

½ teaspoon sea salt

DRESSING
1 teaspoon lemon zest

¼ cup lemon juice

2 tablespoons prepared horseradish

1 tablespoon maple syrup or honey

½ cup olive oil

Salt

Pepper

SALAD
4 cups torn butter lettuce

1 fennel bulb, cored and thinly sliced

1 head radicchio, thinly sliced

½ English cucumber, seeded and cut into ½-inch pieces

½ cup chopped fresh parsley

¼ cup chopped fresh dill

¼ cup chopped fresh basil

¼ cup chopped fresh chives

Moroccan-Spiced Roasted Carrot and Chickpea Salad

SERVES
6

ON THE TABLE IN...
1 hour

Inspired by my travels to Morocco, this spiced carrot salad brings back images of the mountains of rich spices I saw in the markets of Marrakech. The blend of paprika, cinnamon, coriander, cumin, and turmeric helps bring out the natural sweetness of the carrots, along with a drizzle of date syrup and tahini. My twist? I roast the chickpeas with the carrots, which helps them crisp up and become full of flavor. When tossed with the dressing, the chickpeas act like sponges, absorbing the flavors and helping make this salad into a hearty plant-based meal.

7 medium carrots, cut into
   1-by-½-inch pieces

1 (14-oz) can chickpeas, drained
   and rinsed

5 tablespoons olive oil, divided

1½ teaspoons sweet paprika

½ teaspoon ground cinnamon

½ teaspoon ground coriander

½ teaspoon ground cumin

¼ teaspoon ground turmeric

1 teaspoon sea salt, divided

½ teaspoon black pepper,
   plus more as needed

¼ cup chopped almonds

½ small red onion, thinly sliced

1½ tablespoons apple cider
   vinegar

1 teaspoon date syrup,
   plus more as needed

4 cups arugula

¼ cup fresh mint leaves or cilantro

2 tablespoons tahini

Preheat the oven to 400°F. Line a sheet pan with aluminum foil.

Combine the carrots and chickpeas in a bowl. Add 3 tablespoons of the olive oil, paprika, cinnamon, coriander, cumin, turmeric, ½ teaspoon of the salt, and pepper and toss until combined.

Spread out the carrots and chickpeas on the prepared sheet pan. Set the bowl aside to use later. Roast for 25 minutes, or until the carrots are tender. Add the almonds to the pan and roast for an additional 3 to 5 minutes, or until golden.

Meanwhile, in the bowl you set aside, combine the red onion, apple cider vinegar, date syrup, remaining ½ teaspoon salt, and pepper and mix well. Let sit for 5 minutes. Add the remaining 2 tablespoons of olive oil and mix well. This helps reduce the sharpness of the raw onion.

Add the chickpea and carrot mixture to the red onion mixture and toss to combine.

Place the arugula in a serving bowl. Top with the carrot mixture and drizzle any excess dressing over the salad. Top with the mint and drizzle with the tahini and additional date syrup.

NOTE: To prepare in advance, make the carrot mixture and dressing and store separately. Just before serving, toss the carrot mixture and dressing with the arugula, mint, tahini, and date syrup to taste.

HOW TO TEMPER SHARP-FLAVORED ONIONS If you find that raw onions are too sharp or pungent, try soaking them in ice water for 5 to 10 minutes. Drain and add them to your dish. Alternatively, add the sliced raw onion directly to your salad dressing, and let it marinate for 5 to 10 minutes. Toss directly with the salad. This helps soften the sharp flavor while infusing the dressing into the onion.

WHAT IS SUMAC? A spice known for its unique tangy taste and dark red color, sumac is a member of the cashew family. Sumac berries are dried and ground into a powder, not only to consume but also to be used as a dye for wool and leather, as well as for medicinal properties to treat indigestion. Sumac can be found in many specialty spice shops, Middle Eastern grocery stores, online marketplaces, or well-stocked grocery stores.

Beet and Sumac Salad with Oranges

SERVES
4 to 6

ON THE TABLE IN...
1 hour 10 minutes

Beets make a vibrant base for winter salads. With their earthy sweetness, beets are a culinary powerhouse due to their versatility in soups (Fennel and Beet Borscht, page 73), marinades (Vegan Celeriac "Pastrami" Sandwich, page 163), and dips (Beet Baba Ghanoush with Pomegranate, page 116). This lettuce-free salad is packed full of sweet and sour flavors thanks to the beets, dressing, and tangy sumac, a bright red spice that packs a punch. Colorful green pistachios offer visual and textural contrast, along with juicy orange segments, making it almost too pretty to eat. The ingredients in this salad are seasonal, making it great for cooler months.

Preheat the oven to 400°F.

Wrap the beets in foil and place them on a sheet pan or in a baking dish. Bake for 50 to 60 minutes, or until tender. Let them come to room temperature.

Once cooled, rub the beet skin off with a paper towel (use a paring knife if the skin does not easily come off). Cut the beets into ¼-inch wedges and combine them in a serving bowl with the oranges. Hint: If your hands become beet red, try scrubbing with a mixture of baking soda and water.

In a small jar or bowl, combine the orange juice, zest, white wine vinegar, Dijon mustard, honey, and sumac. Season with salt and pepper. While whisking, drizzle in the olive oil.

Drizzle the dressing over the beets and oranges. Top with the pistachios and mint leaves.

- 3 pounds (6 or 7) red beets, tops removed
- 3 oranges, peeled and cut into segments, juice reserved
- ¼ teaspoon orange zest
- 2 tablespoons white wine vinegar
- 1 teaspoon Dijon mustard
- 1 teaspoon honey or agave syrup
- 1½ teaspoons sumac
- Salt
- Pepper
- 2 tablespoons olive oil
- ½ cup shelled chopped pistachios
- ½ cup fresh mint leaves

NOTE: Cook the beets up to 5 days in advance and store them in an airtight container in the refrigerator, or buy precooked, vacuum-sealed beets.

VARIATION: This salad works really well with any citrus, from oranges to grapefruit. For a heartier salad, add cooked lentils or feta.

Smashed Cucumber Dill Salad

SERVES
4 to 6

ON THE TABLE IN...
40 minutes

My zaida (grandfather), named Arnold, was a natural host. Every time we went to his house, he would come in with a tray of candies, Mrs. Fields cookies, Coke, and ice cream floats (with unique flavor combinations, like cream soda or orange soda in place of cola, no less). He made freshly squeezed orange juice for my bubbe (grandmother) every morning, and if you were lucky, he would make you a batch of "Zaida's Pickles," made with pickling cucumbers, salt, sugar, and vinegar. It was a perfectly tangy treat that we looked forward to and craved every summer. Since then, I often make my own pickle variations and think of how he took such pride in caring for others. The flavors of Arnie's pickles inspired me to create this cucumber salad, a modern twist of a side dish that is a hybrid between a salad and a plate of his pickles. It's a great dinner party option.

SALADS, SPREADS & SIDES

2 large English cucumbers
    or 6 Persian cucumbers
½ teaspoon kosher salt,
    plus more as needed
2 tablespoons white wine vinegar
1 teaspoon sugar
1 garlic clove, minced
½ cup chopped fresh dill
Black pepper

Cut the ends off the cucumbers and cut them in half lengthwise. Place the cucumber halves, cut side down, on a cutting board and, using the handle of a wooden spoon or spatula, press down firmly using the heel of your hand until the cucumber splits, repeating the motion along the length of the cucumber. Once it is evenly smashed, cut the cucumbers into diagonal 1-inch slices. Transfer the cucumbers to a large bowl, add the salt, toss until combined, and let sit for 20 minutes.

Using a colander, drain the excess liquid from the cucumbers, and then return them to the bowl. Add the vinegar, sugar, and garlic, toss, and let sit for 10 minutes.

Add the dill and mix until combined. Taste, season with salt and pepper, and serve.

NOTE: This salad gets better the longer it sits. Make it up to 1 day in advance and toss with the fresh dill just before serving.

SUBSTITUTION: Instead of white wine vinegar, try white balsamic vinegar or any white vinegar.

PICKLES AND JEWISH CUISINE Pickles play an important part in Jewish cuisine, especially for those living in Poland, Ukraine, Lithuania, and Russia. Before refrigeration was possible, pickling was a way to preserve fruits and vegetables to ensure there was enough to eat throughout the cold winter months. There are two main types of pickling: with a brine and with vinegar. Salt-brined pickles are what we now associate with Jewish delis because vinegar was too expensive for poor Jews to afford. Jewish home cooks used salt to preserve the summer's bounty along with garlic and dill and were then left to ferment for weeks, if not months.

POMEGRANATES This ancient fruit has a special role in Jewish cuisine. Commonly enjoyed during Rosh Hashanah, pomegranates are thought to contain 613 arils, one for each commandment in the Torah. Additionally, pomegranates are one of the seven species of Israel enjoyed during Tu B'Shvat alongside figs, grapes, barley, wheat, dates, and olives.

Pomegranate Lentil Tabbouleh

SERVES
4 to 6

ON THE TABLE IN...
20 minutes

Tabbouleh is a classic Levantine herb-based salad traditionally made with soaked bulgur wheat, parsley, cucumber, and tomatoes in a simple lemon and olive oil dressing, served alongside falafel and shawarma. While tabbouleh is delicious, I'm always looking to include plant-based protein into my salads to make a one-bowl meal. This modern take on tabbouleh is full of fresh mint, parsley, juicy pomegranate seeds, and hearty lentils. In place of cracked bulgur, I like to use sesame seeds to make this salad grain- and gluten-free.

In a medium bowl, combine the chopped onion, tomato, and cucumber. Season liberally with salt and pepper. Let sit for 5 to 10 minutes. This helps remove excess water from the vegetables.

While the vegetables are salting, combine the parsley, mint, pomegranate arils, and cooked lentils in a serving bowl.

Use a colander to drain the onion and tomato mixture, pressing out any excess liquid. Add the mixture to the serving bowl.

Add the lemon zest, lemon juice, olive oil, sesame seeds, and za'atar and toss to combine. Season with salt and pepper to taste.

NOTE: Make this salad up to 3 days in advance by combining everything but the fresh herbs in an airtight container and refrigerating. Toss with the herbs just before serving.

VARIATIONS: Add 2 teaspoons of ground sumac to this recipe for a tangier variation. Omit the sesame seeds and add hemp seeds for added protein.

½ yellow onion, finely chopped

1 medium tomato, cut into ¼-inch pieces

½ English cucumber, seeded and cut into ¼-inch pieces

Salt

Pepper

2 cups roughly chopped fresh parsley

½ cup roughly chopped fresh mint leaves

½ cup pomegranate arils

½ cup cooked brown or green lentils

1 teaspoon lemon zest

Juice of 1 lemon (about 3 tablespoons)

3 tablespoons olive oil

¼ cup sesame seeds

2 teaspoons za'atar

Vegan Potato Latkes

My uncle Ted (ז״ל) was famous for his latkes, and he swore that his secret was doing everything by hand. In my opinion, they tasted so incredible because they were painstakingly made with love, every year, alongside a shot of slivovitz and a massive bear hug. While making latkes by hand is an option, I like to use my food processor in a pinch to make these. This vegan potato latke recipe is an eggless version of the Hanukkah favorite, bound together with a ground flax egg and fried until golden. I top mine with a vegan sour cream or labneh and a hefty shake of everything bagel spice. Add a whole, trimmed carrot to the frying oil to help keep the oil clean. It acts as a magnet for the potato particles and helps maintain the oil temperature due to its water content. The carrot will burn faster than the potatoes, a small sacrifice to pay for perfect latkes.

2 pounds (about 3 large) russet potatoes, scrubbed

½ medium yellow onion, peeled

3 tablespoons ground flaxseed

2 tablespoons all-purpose flour, gluten-free, if preferred

1 teaspoon potato starch, plus more as needed

½ teaspoon baking powder

1 teaspoon salt

¼ teaspoon black pepper

Vegetable oil, for frying

1 medium carrot, trimmed, for frying

Preheat the oven to 200°F. Line a sheet pan with paper towels. Set aside.

If using a food processor: Quarter the potatoes and cut the onion in half. Attach the shredding disk to the food processor and shred the potatoes and onion. If using a box grater: Grate the potatoes and onion using the largest hole.

Combine the potato and onion on a clean kitchen towel and wrap up tightly. Wring out as much liquid as possible, squeezing it tightly over a sink or bowl to remove the liquid.

Transfer the potato and onion mixture to a large bowl. Add the flaxseed, flour, potato starch, baking powder, salt, and pepper and mix to combine. The potatoes will oxidize and brown quickly, so be sure to prep this right before frying.

Heat ½ inch of oil in a large, heavy, tall-sided skillet over medium-high heat to 360°F to 375°F. It is hot enough if, when you add a small piece of potato to the pan, it sizzles immediately. Add the carrot to the pan. If the latkes aren't holding together, add 2 teaspoons of potato starch to the mixture.

Using a ¼-cup measure, scoop up the latke mixture and pack it in. Add it carefully to the hot oil. You can tap the bottom of the measuring cup with a spatula to release it. Flatten the latke using a spatula. Fry up to 4 latkes at a time, being careful not to overcrowd the skillet. Fry until the bottoms are deep golden brown and crispy, 3 to 4 minutes. Flip the latkes and cook for an additional 3 to 4 minutes.

Use a spatula to transfer the latkes to the prepared sheet pan and keep them warm in the oven until ready to serve. Remove the carrot and discard.

NOTE: To prepare in advance, fry the latkes and place them in a single layer on an ungreased foil-lined sheet pan. Cover with plastic wrap and store in the refrigerator for up to 3 days or in the freezer for up to 3 months. Once frozen, the latkes can be transferred from the sheet pan to a zip-top plastic bag or container. To reheat, bake at 375°F for 7 to 10 minutes or until heated through.

VARIATIONS: Use one sweet potato instead of one of the russet potatoes or try a parsnip for a sweeter latke.

SUBSTITUTION: Use matzo meal in place of all-purpose flour in this recipe if preferred.

HOW TO GET CRISPY LATKES

For a starter, be sure to use starchy russet potatoes. Squeeze the potato and onion mixture in a clean kitchen towel to wring out as much excess liquid as possible. The latke should sizzle immediately when it hits the oil. When frying, use a cast-iron pan or heavy-bottomed pan for even cooking. Be careful not to crowd the pan when cooking.

Crispy Tahdig Rice "Latkes"

SERVES
4

ON THE TABLE IN...
1 hour 15 minutes,
including 15 minutes resting time

While we typically think of latkes as being potato based, this rice-based recipe was inspired by the Persian dish of tahdig and reimagined for Hanukkah. The patties are fried in oil and served like a classic potato latke. It uses sticky sushi rice in place of basmati to help the patties stick together without the help of binding agents like eggs. With the crispy edges of the rice being my favorite, these fried patties are full of rich pistachios, and fragrant saffron, and then topped with a zesty cucumber and cilantro topping.

Make the patties In a liquid measuring cup, combine the saffron threads and hot water. Let sit for 10 minutes.

In a medium saucepan over medium heat, heat the olive oil until hot but not smoking. Add the onion and garlic and cook until they begin to soften, 4 to 5 minutes.

Add the sushi rice and cook for 2 to 3 minutes to toast the rice slightly. Add the saffron water, salt, and currants to the saucepan and bring to a boil. Decrease the heat to a simmer and cook, covered, for 20 minutes, or until all the liquid has been absorbed. Remove from the stove and set aside to cool slightly.

Add the pistachios to the rice and stir to combine.

Line a sheet pan with paper towels. Set aside.

Using a ⅓-cup measure, scoop up the cooled rice into a patty, pressing it firmly to shape into a ½-inch-thick circle. Transfer it to a plate. Repeat with the rest of the rice and transfer them to two plates. Wet your hands to prevent sticking. Refrigerate the rice patties, covered, for 15 minutes.

Make the cucumber cilantro topping In a medium bowl, combine the cucumber, cilantro leaves, lime juice, olive oil, sugar, lime zest, and salt. Set aside.

continued

PATTIES

¼ teaspoon crushed saffron threads

1⅔ cups hot water

1 tablespoon extra-virgin olive oil, plus more for frying

1 medium yellow onion, finely chopped

3 garlic cloves, finely chopped

1 cup sushi rice, rinsed

½ teaspoon sea salt, plus more for sprinkling

2 tablespoons currants

¼ cup shelled finely chopped pistachios

CUCUMBER CILANTRO TOPPING

½ English cucumber, seeded and diced into ¼-inch pieces

½ cup fresh cilantro leaves, lightly packed

2 tablespoons lime juice

4 teaspoons extra-virgin olive oil

½ teaspoon sugar

½ teaspoon lime zest

½ teaspoon sea salt

Fry the patties Heat ½ inch of olive oil in a tall-sided skillet over medium-high heat until it shimmers. To test the temperature, add a small grain of rice to the oil; it should sizzle immediately. Add the rice patties, 3 or 4 at a time, and cook until golden and crispy, about 3 minutes per side. Transfer them to the prepared sheet pan and sprinkle with additional salt.

Serve with the cucumber cilantro topping.

NOTE: To prepare in advance, fry the tahdig latkes, place them in an even layer on an ungreased foil-lined sheet pan, and cover with plastic wrap. Refrigerate for up to 3 days or freeze for up to 3 months. Once frozen, the latkes can be transferred from the sheet pan to an airtight bag or container. To reheat, bake at 375°F for 5 to 8 minutes or until heated through.

VARIATION: If you can't find saffron, use ¼ teaspoon ground turmeric in its place.

WHAT IS TAHDIG?

Tahdig is a Persian dish of crispy, golden rice. *Tahdig* means "bottom of the pot," and the dish gets its signature crunch from the rice cooking at the bottom of the cooking pot. The cooking pot is then inverted onto a plate, revealing a stunning "cake" of crispy, golden rice. It gets its hue from vibrant saffron and is usually flavored with fragrant basmati rice, yogurt, and butter.

Creamy Mamaliga

SERVES
4

ON THE TABLE IN...
15 minutes

Mamaliga is an Eastern European corn porridge, similar to polenta. My bubbe (grandmother) Muriel was of Romanian descent. She loved to tell me stories about how she and her cousin, Ruthie, would make an entire box of mamaliga and use a whole stick of butter, eating the entire thing out of the pot while their husbands and kids were out of the house. This recipe is inspired by Muriel's love for this stick-to-your-ribs dish, with a twenty-first-century twist. It makes a lovely base for the Red Wine-Braised Beets (page 144).

In a medium saucepan, combine the water, milk, and salt and bring to a boil over medium-high heat. Add the polenta and decrease the heat to medium-low. Whisking constantly, cook until the polenta thickens, about 4 minutes. Add the vegan butter, tahini, nutritional yeast, and black pepper and whisk until well combined.

Serve immediately or add 1 to 2 tablespoons of water, as needed, to maintain the desired consistency and texture.

2 cups water

1 cup plain unsweetened non-dairy milk

½ teaspoon salt

1 cup polenta

2 tablespoons unsalted vegan butter

2 tablespoons tahini

3 tablespoons nutritional yeast

½ teaspoon black pepper

NOTE: Mamaliga will solidify and thicken over time. To reheat, combine the mamaliga with a splash of water or non-dairy milk in a pot and whisk over medium heat.

VARIATION: Tahini lends a richness to this dish, but feel free to omit it or substitute with cashew butter.

SUBSTITUTION: This recipe calls for vegan butter and milk, but feel free to use dairy versions if preferred. If you can't find nutritional yeast, use 3 tablespoons of grated Parmesan cheese.

WHAT IS MAMALIGA? Mamaliga is similar to Italian polenta, Bulgarian kachamak, Hungarian puliszka, and Ukrainian kulesha and was commonly known as peasant food in Romanian cuisine. Mamaliga was made over low heat and required constant stirring until it became thick and creamy. It was either eaten as a porridge or made into a hardened "cake," where portions were sliced off and eaten by hand or topped with butter, sour cream, or a sharp sheep's milk cheese—cascaval—which was more common in Romanian cuisine; it was served for breakfast, lunch, or dinner. Leftovers were often cut and fried the next day or cut into slices and served with stews in place of bread.

Carrot and Parsnip Tzimmes with Dates and Pecans

SERVES
6

ON THE TABLE IN...
2 hours

Tzimmes is a traditionally sticky-sweet dish, made of carrots, root vegetables (like sweet potatoes), and dried fruits and baked in a honey and orange juice mixture. It toes the line between dessert and side dish and was always made, but rarely finished, at our family dinners. Instead of a syrupy-sweet side, this spiced, naturally sweetened dish is packed with ginger, pecans, and dates (no prunes here!), resulting in a side dish you'll actually enjoy. I love using multicolored carrots for a visually stunning presentation, but feel free to use whatever carrots you have on hand.

1 medium sweet potato, peeled and cut into 2-by-½-inch-wide wedges

6 medium carrots, cut into 2-by-½-inch pieces

2 medium parsnips, cut into 2-by-½-inch pieces

6 green onions, cut into 2-inch pieces

3 garlic cloves, finely chopped

½ cup dates, pitted and roughly chopped

½ cup pecans, roughly chopped

⅔ cup apple juice

¾ cup vegetable broth, low-sodium if preferred

2 tablespoons maple syrup

2 teaspoons freshly grated ginger

1 teaspoon ground cinnamon

1 teaspoon orange zest

½ teaspoon sea salt

½ teaspoon black pepper

¼ cup unsalted vegan butter, cubed

Flaky salt

Preheat the oven to 350°F.

Combine the sweet potato, carrots, parsnips, green onions, garlic, dates, and pecans in a large baking dish or Dutch oven.

In a small bowl, whisk together the apple juice, vegetable broth, maple syrup, ginger, cinnamon, orange zest, salt, and pepper. Pour the liquid over the vegetable mixture. Top the vegetables with the butter cubes.

Cover the baking dish with a lid or seal tightly with aluminum foil and bake for 60 minutes. Remove the lid or foil and bake for an additional 15 to 20 minutes, or until the vegetables are tender. Sprinkle with flaky salt before serving.

NOTE: Store in an airtight container and refrigerate for up to 4 days or freeze for up to 3 months. Reheat thawed or refrigerated tzimmes at 350°F until warmed through.

VARIATION: Use dried figs in place of the dates if preferred. You may also substitute the pecans with walnuts.

WHAT IS TZIMMES? Tzimmes is a traditional Ashkenazi side dish of root vegetables and dried fruits cooked with honey, spices, and sometimes beef. The word *tzimmes* comes from the Yiddish word "to fuss," because of the endless chopping that goes along with making a pot full of vegetables. Tzimmes is often eaten during the High Holidays and Passover.

Cast-Iron Potato and Caramelized Onion Kugel

SERVES
10 to 12

ON THE TABLE IN...
2 hours

Potato kugel is comfort food at its finest. Kugels, at their core, are baked casseroles. This potato kugel casserole is crisp and golden on the outside and creamy on the inside. It reminds me of a shareable hash brown or a giant latke, and it's served at any time of day (try leftovers at breakfast— really!). Using a preheated cast-iron pan ensures that the kugel is cooked to golden perfection, with everyone getting the best part—the crispy edges! Top your kugel with labneh, sour cream, crème fraîche, or coconut yogurt with chives. Serve with eggs for a breakfast dish or alongside your meal.

5 tablespoons extra-virgin
    olive oil, divided

2 medium yellow onions,
    cut into ½-inch pieces

1½ teaspoons salt, divided

2 pounds (3 or 4) russet potatoes

4 large eggs

½ teaspoon black pepper

¼ cup matzo meal

Sour cream, coconut yogurt,
    crème fraîche, or labneh,
    for serving, optional

Fresh chives, chopped,
    for serving

In a 9-inch cast-iron pan, heat 2 tablespoons of the olive oil over medium heat until the oil is hot but not smoking. Add the chopped onions, spreading them evenly over the bottom of the pan. Decrease the heat to medium-low and let cook, undisturbed, for approximately 10 minutes.

Sprinkle the onions with ½ teaspoon of the salt and cook, stirring occasionally, until browned and broken down, 30 to 45 minutes. Once golden and caramelized, transfer the onions to a large bowl.

Preheat the oven to 350°F.

Add the remaining 3 tablespoons of olive oil to the cast-iron pan and place it in the oven to heat up while you prepare the potatoes.

Fill a large bowl with ice water.

Using a food processor fitted with the shredding disk, or a box grater on the largest hole, grate the potatoes. The potatoes will oxidize, so be sure to shred right before use.

Add the potatoes to the bowl of ice water. Let sit for 10 minutes to remove excess starch.

Drain the potatoes, transfer them to a clean kitchen towel, and wring out any excess liquid. The more liquid you can remove, the better! Add the potatoes to the bowl with the caramelized onions.

Add the remaining 1 teaspoon of salt, eggs, pepper, and matzo meal and stir to combine.

Carefully remove the cast-iron pan from the oven and spread the potato mixture in the pan, pushing it down to compact the potatoes. It should sizzle on contact with the pan. Return the pan to the oven and bake for 1 hour, or until deep golden brown on top.

Serve with sour cream and chopped chives.

NOTE: Prepare this kugel up to 4 days in advance and store in an airtight container in the fridge.

VARIATION: Add ½ cup chopped parsley to the kugel along with the matzo meal.

SUBSTITUTION: This recipe uses russet potatoes, but you can use Idaho potatoes instead.

CARAMELIZING ONIONS These are what give this kugel a rich umami flavor with a hint of sweetness. Caramelizing onions takes time. To speed up the process, try adding ⅛ teaspoon of baking soda to the onions, which will help them brown faster. Caramelized onions can be made up to 3 days in advance, stored in an airtight container, and refrigerated. I like to caramelize a large batch of onions and freeze them in individual containers with about 2 onions' worth in each one.

WHAT IS COCONUT CREAM? You can find canned coconut cream alongside canned coconut milk (in light, sweetened, or full-fat varieties) in the "ethnic" food aisle. When using coconut milk, it is important to note the use of canned coconut milk as opposed to the kind you'll find as a replacement for other non-dairy milks in the refrigerated section of the grocery store. When purchasing canned coconut milk or coconut cream for the recipes in this book, be sure to buy unsweetened, full-fat varieties for the best results. If you can't find coconut cream, purchase two or three cans of full-fat coconut milk and place them in the fridge overnight; when you open the cans, the coconut cream and liquid will have separated. Scoop and measure the coconut cream layer and use it as directed in the recipe. The liquid can be added to smoothies or porridge bowls, or used to cook rice.

Pumpkin Kugel with Pecan Streusel

SERVES	ON THE TABLE IN...	
6	1 hour 10 minutes	

Kugel is Yiddish for "pudding." By definition, kugel is a starchy, baked pudding that contains fat and typically eggs. This version relies on cornstarch for its starch component and rich coconut milk for an ultra-creamy texture. It is anything but traditional, with a soufflé, pudding-like texture that is a mash-up of a sweet potato casserole, kugel, and pumpkin pie. Made with warm spices and topped with a sweet and crunchy pecan streusel, it's a good choice to serve at an autumn Shabbat dinner, Sukkot, or Thanksgiving.

Make the kugel Preheat the oven to 350°F. Generously grease an 8-inch pie dish with cooking spray or coconut oil.

In a medium bowl, whisk together the pumpkin puree, coconut cream, brown sugar, cinnamon, ginger, cardamom, cloves, salt, cornstarch, and baking powder. Pour the pumpkin mixture into the greased pie dish.

Make the topping In a bowl, combine the pecans, flour, brown sugar, coconut oil, cinnamon, and ginger and mix well. Spread it evenly over the kugel.

Bake for 1 hour, or until set. Let cool slightly (it will firm up while cooling).

Top the kugel with whipped cream before serving, if desired.

NOTE: Tightly wrap the kugel (in the pan) with plastic wrap and store in the refrigerator for up to 4 days. To freeze, let cool completely, wrap in a layer of plastic wrap and foil, and freeze for up to 3 months. Reheat in the microwave or the oven at 350°F until heated through.

VARIATION: Use 2½ teaspoons Kafe Hawaij seasoning or pumpkin pie spice in place of the cinnamon, ginger, cardamom, and cloves. If you prefer a less-sweet dish, decrease the sugar to ½ cup.

SUBSTITUTION: Use tapioca starch in place of the cornstarch, if preferred.

KUGEL

1 (29-oz) can pumpkin puree

1 cup canned coconut cream, at room temperature

⅔ cup brown sugar or coconut sugar

1½ teaspoons ground cinnamon

1½ teaspoons ground ginger

½ teaspoon ground cardamom

⅛ teaspoon ground cloves

½ teaspoon sea salt

¼ cup cornstarch or potato starch

½ teaspoon baking powder

PECAN TOPPING

1 cup raw pecans, roughly chopped

¼ cup all-purpose flour, gluten-free, if preferred

3 tablespoons brown sugar or coconut sugar

3 tablespoons coconut oil, melted

½ teaspoon ground cinnamon

¼ teaspoon ground ginger

Whipped cream or vegan whipped cream, for serving (optional)

Beet Baba Ghanoush with Pomegranate

MAKES
2¼ cups

ON THE TABLE IN…
1 hour, including
15 minutes of resting time

Baba ghanoush has always been a favorite dish of mine, but it's one that I used to avoid making at home. The concept of smoking and charring the eggplant felt daunting, messy, and somewhat dangerous… until I learned that you could do it well in advance, over a grill, under a broiler, or in a grill pan. In Israel, baba ghanoush is commonplace at nearly every meal, and it's often made using mayonnaise or yogurt in place of tahini. This recipe plays on that tradition, with a mixture of creamy vegan mayonnaise and nutty tahini swirled with colorful beets and tangy pomegranate molasses for a snackable dip.

1 (1-lb) Italian eggplant

¾ cup chopped cooked beets

¼ cup tahini

2 tablespoons vegan mayonnaise

2 garlic cloves

2 tablespoons pomegranate molasses, plus more for serving

1 teaspoon smoked paprika

¼ teaspoon sea salt

2 to 3 tablespoons extra-virgin olive oil

2 tablespoons pomegranate arils

NOTE: Store baba ghanoush in an airtight container in the refrigerator for up to 5 days or in the freezer for up to 3 months. To cook beets: Boil whole and unpeeled beets in water for 30 minutes. Peel and chop. Roast whole, unpeeled beets, drizzled with olive oil and wrapped in foil, at 400°F for 40 to 60 minutes.

If using a grill or grill pan: Preheat a gas or charcoal grill or grill pan over medium-high heat. Place the eggplant directly on the grill and cook, turning occasionally with tongs, until the eggplant is completely tender, 20 to 30 minutes. Use tongs to remove the eggplant from the grill. Wrap in foil and let sit for 15 minutes.

If using the broiler: Line a sheet pan with foil. Adjust the oven rack to 5 to 6 inches below the broiler. Place the eggplant on the prepared sheet pan and pierce with a fork multiple times. Broil, turning the eggplant occasionally, until charred, 20 to 30 minutes. Wrap in foil and let sit for 15 minutes.

After the eggplant has cooled in the foil, peel the eggplant. The skin should slide off easily after steaming in the foil packet. Transfer the eggplant to a food processor or blender.

Add the beets, tahini, vegan mayonnaise, garlic, pomegranate molasses, smoked paprika, and salt to the food processor. While drizzling in 2 tablespoons of the oil, pulse until well combined but not completely smooth. Pulse in the remaining 1 tablespoon olive oil if the mixture is too thick.

Transfer the mixture to a serving bowl and top with the pomegranate arils and additional pomegranate molasses.

POMEGRANATE MOLASSES Also called pomegranate syrup, this sweet and sour syrup is made of concentrated pomegranate juice. It is delicious in salad dressings, drizzled over roasted vegetables, or even on top of vanilla ice cream.

THE SECRET TO CREAMY HUMMUS

Restaurant hummus is smooth and creamy, because they start with dried beans that are boiled, skinned, and blended until silky smooth. This recipe has a quick but effective shortcut to achieve the smoothest hummus, without needing to peel each individual chickpea. Boil canned chickpeas in water with baking soda to further break down the skins, then skim the skins from the water. You'll have silky-smooth hummus!

Smooth and Creamy Hummus, Four Ways

MAKES
1½ cups

ON THE TABLE IN...
30 minutes

Hummus is a classic dish, and with good reason. While its origin is widely contested, it is an integral part of Israeli and Jewish cuisine. In my opinion, there's no wrong time of day, or way, to enjoy hummus, especially when it's homemade. While buying hummus is convenient, it's easy to make your own at home and you can create nearly endless flavor combinations. With a handful of pantry staples (like canned chickpeas and tahini), homemade hummus comes together in a few minutes for a convenient take on the age-old classic.

In a medium saucepan, combine the chickpeas, water, and baking soda and bring to a boil over medium heat. Decrease the heat to low and simmer for 15 minutes. Drain the chickpeas in a colander and transfer them to a food processor or blender.

Add the lemon juice, garlic, and tahini and blend to combine. With the food processor running, add the ice cube and slowly stream in the olive oil until the hummus is smooth and creamy. Season with salt to taste (I usually use ½ teaspoon).

Everything Bagel Spice: Omit the salt and add 2 to 3 tablespoons Everything Bagel Spice (page 246).

Red Pepper Harissa: Omit the ice cube. Add 1½ teaspoons of harissa and ½ cup of chopped roasted red pepper.

Zhoug: Omit the ice cube and olive oil. Add 3 tablespoons of Zhoug (page 239) or pesto, 1 cup of fresh spinach leaves, and 1 teaspoon of lemon zest.

1 (14-oz) can chickpeas, drained and rinsed

2 cups water

½ teaspoon baking soda

3 tablespoons lemon juice

1 garlic clove

⅓ cup tahini

1 ice cube

¼ cup extra-virgin olive oil

Sea salt

NOTE: Hummus is an easy dish to make ahead. Simply transfer to an airtight container and refrigerate for up to 1 week or freeze for up to 3 months.

VARIATION: This recipe comes with three additional delicious options for customizing your hummus, but get creative and try adding your favorite herb and spice combinations.

SUBSTITUTION: If you can't eat sesame, use Sunflower Tahini (page 238) in place of sesame tahini.

Mains

Savory Pulled Mushroom and Tofu "Brisket"

SERVES	ON THE TABLE IN...	
6	1 hour 30 minutes	

Brisket is synonymous with Jewish cuisine. A fall-apart brisket was the centerpiece of our Hanukkah meal, with umami-rich gravy pooling onto our plates loaded with crispy potato latkes. Recreating the texture and taste of beef for a plant-based dish is challenging, but king trumpet mushrooms and grated tofu help mimic the look and feel of brisket.

"BRISKET"

1½ pounds king trumpet mushrooms

1 (14-oz) block extra-firm tofu

½ cup olive oil

3 tablespoons soy sauce, or gluten-free tamari, if preferred

2 tablespoons smoked paprika

1 tablespoons garlic powder

½ teaspoon black pepper

SAUCE

1 medium yellow onion, peeled and quartered

4 garlic cloves, peeled

2 cups dry red wine

1 cup ketchup

2 tablespoons soy sauce

2 tablespoons Dijon mustard

1 teaspoon dried thyme

1 teaspoon mustard powder

2 tablespoons chopped fresh parsley

VARIATION: For a less traditional, yet very tasty, flavor more similar to a pulled barbecue "beef," in lieu of ketchup, try adding your favorite barbecue sauce.

Preheat the oven to 400°.

Make the "brisket" Use two forks to shred the mushrooms into strips. Put them in a large bowl.

Drain the tofu. Using the largest holes of a box grater, grate the tofu into the bowl with the mushrooms. Add the olive oil, soy sauce, smoked paprika, garlic powder, and pepper and toss with the mushrooms and tofu until well combined.

Transfer the mushroom and tofu mixture to a large rimmed sheet pan and spread it into an even layer. Roast for 30 minutes, or until golden. Set aside.

Make the sauce While the mushrooms are roasting, in a blender or food processor, puree the onion, garlic, red wine, ketchup, soy sauce, Dijon mustard, thyme, and mustard powder until smooth.

Pour the sauce over the roasted mushroom and tofu mixture, stirring until evenly distributed.

Return the sheet pan to the oven and roast for 30 to 35 minutes, stirring halfway through, until the mushrooms and tofu are deep brown. The liquid will evaporate while it roasts, making a thick sauce.

Serve topped with the chopped parsley.

NOTE: Store in airtight containers in the fridge for up to 4 days or in the freezer for up to 3 months.

MUSHROOMS AND PROTEIN Many vegetarian options in restaurants or on the store shelves are mushroom based, from portobello burgers to mushroom jerky. While they are delicious and full of umami-rich flavor, mushrooms are not a replacement for protein and are best served with other protein-rich foods, such as the tofu in this recipe.

Jackfruit and White Bean "Shawarma"

SERVES
4

ON THE TABLE IN...
1 hour 15 minutes

Traditionally made with chicken, beef, or lamb, slow-roasted for hours, and served with tahini sauce, shawarma is a popular street food in Israel. In order to replicate the texture, I've used the mild-tasting and pulled texture of jackfruit to mimic the shaved meat. With a blend of my signature shawarma spices, and slowly roasted with creamy white beans, spicy red onions, and a healthy glug of olive oil, my plant-based version goes well with tahini sauce, amba, tomatoes, and cucumber, on top of hummus, in a pita or malawach wrap, or on top of a salad.

Preheat the oven to 375°F.

In a medium bowl, shred the jackfruit using two forks. Alternatively, add to the bowl of a stand mixer and mix on low, using the mixing paddle to shred. Add the beans, red onion, garlic, olive oil, spice blend, and salt and stir to combine.

Transfer to an 8-by-8-inch baking dish and bake, stirring halfway through, for 1 hour or until somewhat dried and golden.

Serve in a pita, on top of salad, on top of hummus, or with a drizzle of toum.

1 (20-oz) can young jackfruit in brine, drained

1 (14-oz) can white beans, drained and rinsed

1 medium red onion, halved and thinly sliced into half-moons

3 garlic cloves, roughly chopped

⅓ cup extra-virgin olive oil

3 tablespoons Shawarma Spice Blend (page 244)

½ teaspoon sea salt

Pita bread, Smooth and Creamy Hummus, Four Ways (page 119), salad, or Garlic Toum (page 240), for serving

NOTE: Store in an airtight container in the fridge for up to 5 days or in the freezer for up to 3 months.

VARIATION: Use chickpeas in place of the white beans. If you have a shawarma spice blend on hand, use it in the same quantities.

JACKFRUIT Native to Southeast Asia, jackfruit can be enjoyed raw or cooked. Mature jackfruit is bright yellow in color and tastes like a combination of banana, mango, and pineapple. When young, it can be used in place of meat due to its mild flavor and stringy texture. Young jackfruit is typically found canned in brine and mimics the texture of pulled beef or pork but does not contribute significant dietary protein.

Sesame Tofu "Schnitzel"

SERVES	ON THE TABLE IN…	
4	50 minutes	

Every summer, my sister and I would spend ten days at "camp grandma and grandpa" in Vancouver, Canada. Our first meal upon arrival was almost always chicken schnitzel, beaten until paper thin, dredged with cornflake crumbs, and fried in oil. It was a rite of passage to indulge in my grandmother Eva's schnitzel, and I can still taste it, decades later. This vegan version uses extra-firm tofu in place of the chicken, sliced into thin "cutlets," marinated in pickle brine, and coated with a mixture of crunchy panko, rich sesame seeds, and nutty nutritional yeast.

1 (14-oz) block extra-firm tofu

1 cup pickle brine from jarred dill pickles

⅓ cup cornstarch or potato starch

1 teaspoon garlic powder

½ teaspoon smoked paprika

½ cup panko breadcrumbs, gluten-free if preferred

¼ cup sesame seeds

3 tablespoons nutritional yeast

¼ teaspoon sea salt, plus more for sprinkling

2 tablespoons extra-virgin olive oil

2 tablespoons vegan butter or additional olive oil

Lemon wedges, for serving

VARIATION: If you eat tofu during Passover, substitute the panko breadcrumbs with matzo meal for a Passover-friendly version.

Cut the tofu into 8 (½-inch) "steaks." Transfer to a baking dish and spread out in a single layer. Pour the pickle brine over the top and let marinate for 25 minutes, flipping the tofu halfway through if it is not fully submerged.

Drain the tofu from the pickle brine and reserve ⅓ cup of the liquid. Blot the tofu dry with a paper towel.

In a shallow bowl, use a fork to whisk together the cornstarch, reserved brine, garlic powder, and smoked paprika.

In a second shallow bowl, combine the panko breadcrumbs, sesame seeds, nutritional yeast, and salt.

Dip the tofu "steaks" into the cornstarch mixture, flipping to coat on all sides. Dip into the bread crumb mixture, pressing firmly to coat on all sides. Place them on a plate.

Heat the olive oil and vegan butter in a skillet over medium heat. Add the tofu cutlets and fry until golden, 5 to 6 minutes per side. I find it helpful to use two spatulas to flip them over—they are delicate, but they will firm up once cooked.

Transfer the cooked tofu to a cooling rack and sprinkle with salt.

Serve immediately with lemon wedges.

NOTE: Schnitzel is best enjoyed the same day it's made. If you do have leftovers, reheat on an aluminum foil–lined sheet pan at 400°F for 8 to 10 minutes, flipping them halfway through.

WHAT IS SCHNITZEL?

Schnitzel is a dish made of thinly sliced, tenderized meat that is breaded and fried. In Israel, chicken or turkey schnitzel is commonly coated with breadcrumbs and sesame seeds and seasoned with paprika before frying. It is served in sandwiches or alongside french fries, rice, or salad. Schnitzel made its way to Israel via Ashkenazi Jews.

Tempeh and Artichoke "Marbella"

SERVES
6

ON THE TABLE IN...
3 hours 10 minutes, including
2 hours marinating time

Inspired by a recipe for chicken Marbella in the Silver Palate Cookbook *that was published back in the 1980s, this recipe is a hearty main dish packed with flavor. While it bears the name of a coastal Spanish town, it is actually a common dish served in many North American homes for the Jewish New Year and Passover. Every Rosh Hashanah, my mom would serve the iconic chicken dish, a sweet and salty combination of prunes, capers, wine, and chicken thighs. This version uses one of my favorite plant-based proteins—tempeh—and is packed with briny artichokes, dried figs, za'atar, maple syrup, and green olives. I love serving it with couscous, roasted potatoes, or steamed brown rice.*

In a 9-by-13-inch baking dish, combine the tempeh, artichoke hearts, garlic, lemon, white wine, olive oil, red wine vinegar, maple syrup, figs, olives, capers, za'atar, and bay leaves. Cover and marinate for at least 2 hours, or place in the refrigerator and marinate for up to 3 days.

Preheat the oven to 350°F. Let the baking dish come up to room temperature while heating the oven.

Bake for 45 to 50 minutes, or until the tempeh is golden and the sauce has thickened slightly. The figs should be plump.

Transfer to a serving dish, remove the bay leaves, and sprinkle with the chopped parsley.

2 (8-oz) packages tempeh, cut into 16 triangles (8 per package)
1 (14-oz) can artichoke hearts, drained and quartered
5 garlic cloves, finely chopped
2 lemons, cut into ¼-inch slices
¾ cup white wine
½ cup olive oil
⅓ cup red wine vinegar
¼ cup maple syrup
⅔ cup dried figs, quartered
½ cup pitted Spanish green olives, halved
¼ cup capers
2 tablespoons za'atar
2 bay leaves
¼ cup chopped fresh parsley

NOTE: Store leftovers in an airtight container for up to 5 days. Reheat leftovers in the oven at 350°F until warmed through.

VARIATION: If preferred, replace the tempeh with a 14-oz package of extra-firm tofu.

SUBSTITUTIONS: Substitute honey for the maple syrup. Use white wine vinegar in place of red wine vinegar. Use dates in place of dried figs.

Sweet Potato and Sage Vareniki with Hazelnuts

SERVES	ON THE TABLE IN...	
4 to 6; makes 18 to 20 vareniki	1 hour 30 minutes, including 15 minutes resting time	

My great-grandmother Freda emigrated from Ukraine to Canada as a young girl, fleeing the pogroms in the early twentieth century. She brought her family recipes, one of them being vareniki stuffed with potatoes and onion. Freda would travel by bus with a casserole dish, wrapped securely in a tea towel, to share her vareniki with family. If she couldn't be there in person to celebrate the holidays, she would send a tea towel–wrapped dish on the bus, unaccompanied, to be picked up at the bus station upon reaching its destination. This recipe is inspired by hers, but made with flavors of cozy autumn, including fragrant sage, nutty hazelnuts, creamy sweet potato, and sweet maple syrup.

FILLING

12 ounces (about 2) sweet potatoes, peeled and cut into 1-inch pieces

5 ounces (about 3) medium carrots, cut into ½-inch pieces

4 garlic cloves, peeled

1 tablespoon maple syrup

1 tablespoon extra-virgin olive oil

1 teaspoon dried rosemary

½ teaspoon dried thyme

½ teaspoon sea salt

¼ teaspoon Aleppo pepper or red chili flakes

¼ teaspoon black pepper

DOUGH

2 cups all-purpose flour

1 tablespoon cornstarch

½ teaspoon sea salt

½ to ¾ cup water

2 tablespoons extra-virgin olive oil

continued

Make the filling In a medium saucepan, combine the potatoes, carrots, and garlic and add enough water to cover the vegetables by 1 inch. Bring to a boil over medium heat and cook until the potatoes and carrots are fork-tender, 10 to 15 minutes. Drain in a colander.

Transfer the potato, carrot, and garlic to a food processor. Add the maple syrup, oil, rosemary, thyme, salt, Aleppo pepper, and black pepper and pulse into a smooth mixture. Alternatively, mash well using a fork or potato masher. Set aside.

Make the dough Combine the flour, cornstarch, salt, ½ cup water, and olive oil in a bowl or food processor and mix or pulse until a dough forms. Add more water, 1 tablespoon at a time, as needed to form a soft dough. It should be slightly tacky, but not sticky. Cover in plastic wrap and refrigerate for 15 minutes.

Assemble the vareniki Combine the cornstarch and water in a small bowl.

On a lightly floured surface, roll the dough to ⅛ inch thick. Using a drinking glass or biscuit cutter, cut the dough into 3-inch circles.

continued

TO ASSEMBLE
1 tablespoon cornstarch
¼ cup water

TO SERVE
2 tablespoons extra-virgin olive oil
1 medium onion, cut into ½-inch pieces
¼ cup hazelnuts, chopped
⅓ cup fresh sage leaves
Sea salt
Pepper

Gather the scraps and reroll as many times as needed to use up all the dough.

Dip your finger into the cornstarch mixture and run it around the edges of each circle of dough.

Spoon 1 teaspoon of filling in the middle of a circle. Note: Overfilling the vareniki will cause them to burst when cooked. Fold into a half-moon, stretching the dough as needed to cover the filling. Crimp the edges using your thumb, pointer finger, and middle finger. Alternatively, use a fork to crimp. Set the vareniki aside and repeat with the rest of the dough and filling.

Generously grease a sheet pan with olive oil. Set aside.

Bring a large pot of salted water to boil. Cook the vareniki in the boiling water until they float to the surface, 3 to 4 minutes. Remove them with a slotted spoon and transfer to the oiled tray.

To serve Heat the olive oil in a skillet over medium heat. Once shimmering, add the onion and hazelnuts. Sauté until the onions are translucent, 4 to 5 minutes.

Add the vareniki and fry until golden, 3 to 4 minutes per side. Add the sage and toss to combine. Season with salt and pepper before serving.

A DUMPLING BY ANY OTHER NAME
Many cultures have their own variation of the dumpling, from pelmeni (Russia) and pierogies (Poland) to gyoza (Japan). In Ukrainian cuisine, vareniki are traditional dumplings, filled with meat, cheese, potatoes, or a sweet fruit filling. Pierogies and vareniki are similar in that they both are shaped into half-moons and stuffed with a range of fillings, whereas pelmeni are typically smaller, round, and stuffed with meat, which is cooked along with the dough.

NOTE: Cooked vareniki can be stored in an airtight container for up to 1 week. Reheat in the microwave or with olive oil in a frying pan. To freeze, assemble uncooked vareniki on a floured or oiled sheet pan and freeze. Once frozen and solid, transfer to a zip-top freezer bag. Cook directly from frozen in boiling water.

VARIATION: Use walnuts or pecans in place of hazelnuts, if preferred.

Kasha and Mushroom Cabbage Rolls

SERVES
6; makes 12 to 14 cabbage rolls

ON THE TABLE IN...
2 hours 30 minutes

When I was young, my grandmother would make stuffed cabbage filled with spiced beef and rice for almost any occasion. Polish and Romanian cabbage rolls traditionally contain a blend of meats and grains, whereas Ukrainian variations are typically vegetarian with a mixture of grains (like buckwheat) and vegetables (mushrooms) in a sweet and savory sauce. Not only was cabbage commonplace at our holiday dinners, but buckwheat, or kasha, was also a frequently made side dish—so much so that at four years old, I wanted to name our family dog Buckwheat. Spoiler alert: My current dog bears the same name.

Make the cabbage rolls In a small saucepan with a lid, bring the water, 1 tablespoon of the olive oil, and ½ teaspoon of the salt to a boil. Add the rinsed kasha and bring to a simmer. Cover and cook until the water is absorbed, 12 to 14 minutes. Remove from the heat and let sit, covered, for 5 to 10 minutes. Fluff with a fork and transfer to a large bowl to cool.

Meanwhile, in a large skillet over medium heat, add the chopped mushrooms. Cook, stirring often, until they begin to brown and release their liquid, 8 to 12 minutes.

Add the remaining 2 tablespoons of olive oil, onion, garlic, and walnuts and cook until the onion begins to soften, 6 to 8 minutes. Add the red wine, cranberries, soy sauce, and parsley and cook until fragrant, 2 to 3 minutes.

Add the mixture to the cooked and cooled buckwheat and stir to combine. Let cool to room temperature.

Add the ground flax seeds, marjoram, nutmeg, chili flakes, remaining ½ teaspoon of salt, and pepper to the buckwheat mixture and stir to combine.

continued

CABBAGE ROLLS

1¼ cups water

3 tablespoons extra-virgin olive oil, divided

1 teaspoon sea salt, divided

¾ cup kasha or toasted buckwheat, rinsed

12 ounces brown mushrooms, roughly chopped

1 medium yellow onion, chopped

6 garlic cloves, finely chopped

½ cup chopped walnuts

½ cup dry red wine

½ cup dried cranberries

2 teaspoons soy sauce, or gluten-free tamari, if preferred

½ cup chopped fresh parsley

¼ cup ground flax seeds

½ teaspoon dried marjoram

¼ teaspoon ground nutmeg

¼ teaspoon red chili flakes

1 teaspoon black pepper

1 large (or 2 small) green cabbage, stem trimmed

continued

Bring a large pot of water to simmer over medium heat. Add the cabbage and boil until the outer leaves are easily pulled off the core, 4 to 5 minutes Set aside 14 to 16 leaves. If the cabbage leaves are still too difficult to peel off, add the cabbage back to the water to simmer for 4 to 5 minutes longer.

Make the sauce In a medium bowl, combine the crushed tomatoes, tomato sauce, water, soy sauce, maple syrup, apple cider vinegar, paprika, garlic powder, chili flakes, salt, and pepper.

Assemble the rolls Preheat the oven to 350°F. Generously grease a 9-by-13-inch baking dish with olive oil.

Pour a thin layer of sauce on the bottom of the baking dish. Set aside.

Place 1 cabbage leaf in front of you, with the rib side facing up and smooth side down. If the cabbage rib is too large, trim it using a paring knife. Place a scant ⅓ cup of the buckwheat and mushroom mixture 1 inch from the base of the leaf and roll it toward the top. Tuck the sides inward and roll up tightly. Set aside on a plate and repeat with all the cabbage leaves and filling. If some leaves break, roll two together to cover the holes.

Arrange the cabbage rolls in the baking dish in a single layer. Top with the remaining sauce. Cover with aluminum foil and bake for 75 to 90 minutes, or until the cabbage is tender.

Garnish with the chopped parsley, if desired, and serve with sour cream on the side.

NOTE: You can freeze unbaked cabbage rolls. To cook, thaw them in the refrigerator for 30 to 45 minutes, and then bake per the recipe instructions. For even cooking, cover with foil.

VARIATION: Use 2 cups of cooked brown lentils instead of the mushrooms.

SAUCE

1 (14-oz) can crushed tomatoes

1 (14-oz) can tomato sauce

¼ cup water

1 tablespoon soy sauce, or gluten-free tamari, if preferred

1 tablespoon maple syrup

3 tablespoons apple cider vinegar

1 tablespoon Hungarian paprika

½ teaspoon garlic powder

¼ teaspoon red chili flakes

½ teaspoon sea salt

½ teaspoon black pepper

TO SERVE

¼ cup chopped fresh parsley (optional)

½ cup sour cream, coconut yogurt, or labneh

THE SYMBOLISM OF STUFFED FOODS

During the holiday of Simchat Torah, it is customary to eat "stuffed foods," and in many households this means stuffed cabbage. Simchat Torah celebrates the closing of the Torah and the start of a new "cycle." It falls after the seven days of Sukkot. There are several theories as to why stuffed cabbage rolls have become a significant food during this celebration, one being that we are meant to "stuff" the sukkah with our friends, family, and neighbors, so stuffed foods represent coming together in one place. Another is that two rolls side by side resemble the torah scrolls.

Tahini Mac and Cheese Noodle Kugel

SERVES
8

ON THE TABLE IN...
1 hour 20 minutes

There's nothing more comforting than macaroni and cheese. Hearty noodles, covered in creamy, cheesy sauce and topped with herbed breadcrumbs is one of my go-to comfort meals. Growing up, macaroni and cheese meant a bright blue box of Kraft Dinner (which is what Kraft Macaroni and Cheese is called in Canada), and kugel was made with sweet raisins, sour cream, and crispy cornflakes. This Tahini Mac and Cheese Noodle Kugel marries my childhood comfort classic and the quintessential Jewish noodle kugel, with a nutty twist and an abundance of rich smoked Gouda.

KUGEL

1 pound wide egg noodles

5 large eggs

2 cups cottage cheese

⅓ cup tahini

1½ cups (12 oz) shredded mild Cheddar cheese

2 cups (16 oz) shredded smoked Gouda

¼ teaspoon ground nutmeg

TOPPING

¾ cup panko breadcrumbs

2 tablespoons sesame seeds

2 tablespoons tahini

¼ cup unsalted butter, melted

1 teaspoon garlic powder

1 teaspoon smoked paprika

¼ teaspoon sea salt

Preheat the oven to 350°F. Generously grease a 9-by-13-inch baking dish with olive oil or cooking spray.

Make the kugel Cook the egg noodles according to the package directions until al dente, 6 to 7 minutes. Drain and set aside. Let cool slightly.

In a large bowl, combine the eggs, cottage cheese, tahini, Cheddar cheese, smoked Gouda, and nutmeg. Add the cooled noodles to the cheese mixture and mix until combined. Transfer to the greased baking dish.

Make the topping In a medium bowl, combine the panko breadcrumbs, sesame seeds, tahini, melted butter, garlic powder, smoked paprika, and salt and mix well.

Top the noodle mixture with the bread crumb mixture and bake for 40 to 50 minutes, or until golden.

Remove from the oven and let cool slightly before slicing.

NOTE: Store leftover kugel in airtight containers in the fridge for up to 5 days. Wrap cooked kugel in plastic wrap and foil and freeze for up to 3 months. Reheat in the oven at 350°F until warmed through. I like to drizzle more tahini on top of my kugel when I eat it as leftovers for added moisture.

VARIATIONS: Use breadcrumbs or cornflakes in place of the panko breadcrumbs. Smoked Gouda lends a lovely, rich flavor, but you can use mozzarella or Gruyère, plus 1 teaspoon of smoked paprika, for similar results.

WHAT IS KUGEL? This traditional Ashkenazi casserole is often served during the High Holidays, Passover, Shabbat, and Sukkot. Kugels can be sweet or savory, made with potatoes, noodles, or starchy vegetables. Potato kugel is common during Passover, and noodle kugels are found on Rosh Hashanah and break-fast menus. Despite potatoes and noodles being the standard base of kugels, they can be made with any starch (see Pumpkin Kugel with Pecan Streusel, page 115).

Cheesy Jumbo Stuffed Kasha and Shells

SERVES	ON THE TABLE IN...	
8	1 hour 30 minutes	

Kasha, or buckwheat groats, has been a staple in my diet since I was young. I remember going to Eastern European grocery stores to source a specific brand of kasha—Wolff's—that my great-grandmother Freda used, and coming back to watch my mom make kasha and shells for holidays. From toasting the kasha in schmaltz and an egg "until it's done," and then cooking it, it felt like a ritual that couldn't be rushed. I fell so in love with kasha, in fact, that my dog bears the name Buckwheat. Instead of the classic dish of kasha, fried onions, and bow ties or shell pasta, I've made it into a family-style dish that is a hybrid between the traditional and a lasagna—it's layered and stuffed with mushrooms, Parmesan, and mozzarella cheese and baked into a family-style casserole.

4 tablespoons extra-virgin olive oil, divided

2 medium yellow onions, diced into ¼-inch pieces

2 pounds brown mushrooms, stems removed, roughly chopped

5 garlic cloves, chopped

1 cup kasha

2 cups low-sodium vegetable broth

12 ounces jumbo shell pasta

2 large eggs

¾ cup grated Parmesan cheese

½ teaspoon sea salt

1 teaspoon ground black pepper

2 cups grated mozzarella cheese

Preheat the oven to 400°F. Generously grease an 11-inch oval baking dish or a 9-by-13-inch baking dish.

Heat 2 tablespoons of the olive oil in an oven-safe skillet over medium-high heat. Add the diced onions and cook until they begin to brown, 6 to 8 minutes. Add the mushrooms and garlic and cook, stirring occasionally, until browned and the liquid has evaporated, 12 to 15 minutes. Transfer half the mushroom mixture to a large bowl and spread out the remaining mushroom mixture in the skillet.

Meanwhile, rinse the kasha in a colander under running water. In a medium saucepan, heat the remaining 2 tablespoons of olive oil over medium heat. Add the kasha and cook until toasted and fragrant, 3 to 4 minutes.

Pour in the vegetable broth and bring the mixture to a boil. Lower the heat to a simmer, cover, and cook until the liquid is completely absorbed and the kasha is cooked, 15 to 20 minutes. Transfer to the large bowl with the mushroom mixture. Let cool slightly. Rinse the pot—it can be used to cook the shells.

Meanwhile, fill a large pot with salted water and bring to a boil. Cook the shells according to the package directions. Drain and drizzle lightly with oil to prevent sticking.

Once the kasha mixture has cooled slightly, add the eggs, Parmesan cheese, salt, and pepper and mix until well combined.

Scoop 1 tablespoon of the kasha mixture into each shell. Arrange the stuffed shells on top of the mushrooms in the skillet and top with the shredded mozzarella cheese.

Bake for 20 minutes, or until the cheese has melted.

NOTE: To freeze, assemble the dish, unbaked, and wrap the baking dish with plastic wrap and foil. Before baking, unwrap, bring the dish to room temperature, and bake as usual. Leftovers can be stored in an airtight container for up to 5 days. Reheat in the microwave.

VARIATION: You can also try layering this between lasagna sheets instead of shells. For a dairy-free version, substitute the Parmesan cheese with nutritional yeast and top with vegan mozzarella cheese.

SUBSTITUTION: Use lactose-free or non-dairy cheese, if preferred.

KASHA Also called buckwheat, this seed has been a staple in Ashkenazi Jewish cuisine for centuries. It grows exceptionally well in northeastern Europe and can be stored during cold, winter months. When Eastern European Jews immigrated to North America, they brought their love for kasha with them and continued to include it in their diets. Kasha varnishkes started as a dish that resembles a vareniki or pierogi more than it does the bow-tie or shell-shaped pasta we are accustomed to serving with kasha and came about largely because of the widely available boxed, dried pasta found in North America.

WHAT IS CHRAIME?

A common dish among Mizrahi and Sephardic Jews, chraime is often served for Friday-night Shabbat dinner, Rosh Hashanah, and Passover. It is typically made with a whitefish poached in a tomato broth and is packed with aromatic spices. The word *chraime* has roots in the Arabic word meaning "hot." In Sephardic families, chraime is often served in lieu of gefilte fish during Passover.

Spiced Cauliflower Chraime

SERVES
4

ON THE TABLE IN...
1 hour

Chraime is a spicy North African fish stew and a popular Sephardic recipe during Rosh Hashanah, Passover, and Shabbat. This vegan version highlights cauliflower, stewed until tender, studded with plump and juicy golden raisins. Drizzled with date syrup, this sweet and spicy tomato-based stew is a great weeknight meal. Cauliflower takes on the flavor (and color) of the vibrant spices, making it a stunning centerpiece for your meal. Serve the chraime over couscous, rice, or quinoa or with Sesame Seed Malawach (page 208).

Heat the olive oil in a deep skillet over medium heat. Add the onion and cook until it begins to soften, 5 to 6 minutes.

Add the garlic, tomato paste, smoked paprika, turmeric, coriander, cumin, ginger, cinnamon, chili flakes, and salt, stir until combined, and cook for 2 to 3 minutes. Pour in the lemon juice, canned tomatoes, broth, and raisins and stir to combine.

Place the cauliflower in the pan, cut side down in a single layer. Bring the liquid to a boil, decrease the heat to a simmer, cover, and cook until the cauliflower is tender, 15 to 20 minutes.

Drizzle with the date syrup and garnish with the cilantro. Serve with cooked couscous or rice.

NOTE: Store in an airtight container in the fridge for up to 5 days. Reheat in a pan, oven, or microwave until warmed through.

VARIATIONS: Substitute chopped dried apricots or figs instead of raisins. Looking for more protein? Add a can of drained and rinsed chickpeas along with the canned tomatoes and/or crumble some feta cheese on top.

2 tablespoons extra-virgin olive oil

½ medium white onion, cut into ½-inch pieces

3 garlic cloves, finely chopped

3 tablespoons tomato paste

4 teaspoons smoked paprika

2 teaspoons ground turmeric

1 teaspoon ground coriander

1 teaspoon ground cumin

1 teaspoon ground ginger

¼ teaspoon ground cinnamon

½ teaspoon red chili flakes

¼ teaspoon sea salt

Juice of 1 lemon (about 2 tablespoons)

½ cup canned diced tomatoes

1¼ cups vegetable broth, low-sodium if preferred

½ cup golden raisins

1 small head cauliflower, cut into 6 wedges (if using a large cauliflower, cut into 8 wedges)

2 teaspoons date syrup or maple syrup

½ cup chopped fresh cilantro, for serving

Cooked couscous or rice, for serving

Red Wine-Braised Beets with Creamy Mamaliga

SERVES
4

ON THE TABLE IN...
1 hour 15 minutes

There's something to be said about a plant-based main dish that showcases seasonal produce, without forcing it to replicate an animal-based dish. This recipe achieves just that—it is a hearty main dish that stands on its own, no meat in sight. Inspired by the red wine–braised briskets served at holiday meals, these beets are full of complex flavor. Sweet, sour, and somewhat earthy, they pair beautifully with a rich and creamy mamaliga. Make the mamaliga while the beets are simmering and reheat before serving.

2 pounds (6 or 7) beets, scrubbed

1¼ cups dry red wine

½ cup water or vegetable broth, low-sodium if preferred

1 shallot, quartered

1 bay leaf

1 sprig fresh rosemary

½ teaspoon salt

½ teaspoon black pepper, plus more as needed

¼ cup sherry vinegar

2 tablespoons maple syrup

Creamy Mamaliga (page 107)

NOTE: Prepare the beets and mamaliga up to 3 days in advance and store them separately in airtight containers in the refrigerator.

Trim the ends of the beets. If the beet greens are attached, remove them. Cut the beets in half lengthwise. If the beets are large, cut them into quarters. Place the halved beets, cut side down, in a deep skillet with a lid.

Add the red wine, water, shallot, bay leaf, rosemary, salt, and pepper to the skillet and bring to a boil over medium-high heat. Once boiling, decrease the heat to low, cover, and simmer until the beets are tender and can be pierced easily with a fork or paring knife, 40 to 50 minutes. Using tongs, transfer the beets to a cutting board and let cool.

Increase the heat to medium-high and cook, stirring frequently, until the cooking liquid reduces by half, 5 to 6 minutes.

Add the sherry vinegar and maple syrup and cook, stirring constantly, until it thickens and reduces to a glaze, 1 to 2 minutes. When pulling the spoon through, it should leave a wide trail that slowly fills back in. Remove the skillet from the heat. Use tongs to remove the bay leaf and rosemary and discard.

Once the beets have cooled, rub the skin off with a paper towel. Use a paring knife if the skin does not easily come off. Cut the beets into wedges about ½ inch wide, return them to the skillet with the glaze, and toss to coat.

Serve the beets on top of the mamaliga. Top with freshly ground black pepper.

USE THE BEET GREENS!
While this recipe doesn't call for beet greens, they are a fantastic addition to your meal. If your beets have greens, roughly chop them and sauté lightly with some minced garlic, olive oil, and a squeeze of lemon juice. Chopped beet greens are also great in pasta or lasagna.

WHAT IS GEFILTE? *Gefilte* means "stuffed fish" in Yiddish, and this traditional food refers to its origins (before becoming a poached fish ball) when, historically, it was a mixture of fish, breadcrumbs, eggs, and vegetables that were stuffed into a fish skin and cooked. It was a dish that was inspired by scarcity and the repurposing of ingredients. Not only was it an economical dish, but it was also forbidden to debone fish during Shabbat, so this boneless fish dish was ideal for eating during the Sabbath.

Vegan "Gefilte" Cakes

MAKES
10 cakes

ON THE TABLE IN...
1 hour, including
10 minutes resting time

*Gefilte fish is a delicacy in my family; my great-grandmother Freda was famous for her recipe.
My mom and grandmother spent years trying to replicate it, which was passed down verbally
with measurements of handfuls and a bisl ("a bit"). Finally, they were able to nail it down.
I couldn't make a Jewish cookbook without paying homage to this family tradition. I made
a vegan recipe using a mixture of vegetables, seaweed, and spices to mimic the flavor and
textures of Freda's gefilte.*

Preheat the oven to 350°F. Line a sheet pan with parchment paper.

In a food processor, pulse the chopped carrot, cauliflower, parsnip, potato, and onion until they are the size of peas. Add the cashews to the food processor and pulse until they are the size of rice.

Transfer the vegetables to a medium bowl. Add the nori, matzo meal, flax meal, water, pepper, salt, lemon zest, potato starch, and baking powder and mix until combined. Let sit for 10 minutes.

Using a ¼-cup measure, form the mixture into 10 patties. Transfer them to a plate and refrigerate for 10 minutes.

Heat the olive oil in a nonstick pan over medium-high heat. Cook the patties until golden, 3 to 4 minutes per side. Transfer the patties to the prepared sheet pan and bake for 15 minutes. Sprinkle with flaky sea salt.

Meanwhile, cut the remaining carrot into ¼-inch slices. Combine the carrots and enough water to cover by 1 inch in a medium saucepan and bring to a boil over medium-high heat. Lower the heat to a simmer and gently cook the carrots until tender. Drain and set aside.

Top the patties with the sliced carrot and serve with horseradish.

- 2 medium carrots, scrubbed, 1 roughly chopped
- ¼ head cauliflower, cut into florets
- 1 medium parsnip, peeled and roughly chopped
- 1 medium russet potato, peeled and roughly chopped
- ¼ white onion, roughly chopped
- ¼ cup raw cashews
- 1 sheet sushi nori, finely chopped
- ¼ cup matzo meal
- 3 tablespoons flax meal
- ¼ cup water
- ½ teaspoon black pepper
- ½ teaspoon sea salt
- 1 teaspoon lemon zest
- 1 teaspoon potato starch
- ½ teaspoon baking powder
- ¼ cup extra-virgin olive oil
- Flaky sea salt, for serving
- Horseradish, for serving

VARIATION: You can substitute nori with 1 tablespoon dulse flakes, 2 tablespoons furikake seasoning, or 2 tablespoons kelp granules.

NOTE: The gefilte cakes can be frozen for up to 3 months and reheated on an aluminum foil–lined sheet pan in the oven at 400°F until heated through.

Dukkah-Crusted Fried Cauliflower "Steaks"

SERVES	ON THE TABLE IN...		
4	1 hour		

The trick to tender cauliflower "steaks" is to prebake the cauliflower and then add the coating, which prevents the coating from burning. Made with matzo meal, this Passover-friendly main dish is suitable all year-round. I like to serve these with a topping of labneh or rich coconut yogurt and a drizzle of olive oil, parsley, and lemon juice.

2 small heads cauliflower, stems trimmed and leaves removed

½ teaspoon sea salt, plus more as needed

3 large eggs

½ cup plain unsweetened almond milk

1 cup matzo meal

½ cup Dukkah (page 243) or store-bought

¼ cup sesame seeds

1 teaspoon lemon zest

1 teaspoon garlic powder

¼ teaspoon pepper

⅓ cup cornstarch or potato starch

6 tablespoons extra-virgin olive oil, divided

1 cup labneh or coconut yogurt, for serving

¼ cup chopped fresh parsley, for serving

1 lemon, cut into wedges, for serving

SUBSTITUTION: Check your store-bought dukkah to ensure it is Passover-friendly. If not, make the recipe on page 243.

Preheat the oven to 425°F. Line a sheet pan with parchment paper.

Cut the cauliflower into 1-inch "steaks," keeping the core intact. Reserve any excess florets. Arrange the cauliflower in a single layer on the prepared sheet pan, salt generously, and bake for 15 to 20 minutes.

Meanwhile, whisk the eggs and almond milk in a shallow dish. In a separate shallow dish, combine the matzo meal, dukkah, sesame seeds, lemon zest, garlic powder, ½ teaspoon salt, and pepper. Lastly, place the cornstarch in a third shallow dish.

Remove the cauliflower from the oven and let cool slightly. Dip a cauliflower steak into the cornstarch, then into the eggs, and then coat with the matzo meal dukkah mixture. Repeat with all the cauliflower pieces and place them on a plate.

Generously grease the prepared sheet pan with 3 tablespoons of the olive oil. Place the breaded cauliflower onto the sheet pan in one layer and bake for 10 minutes. Flip the cauliflower and drizzle with the remaining 3 tablespoons of olive oil. Bake for an additional 10 minutes.

Serve on top of labneh, garnished with the chopped parsley and lemon wedges.

NOTE: To reheat, place on a sheet pan lined with aluminum foil and bake at 400°F for 5 minutes.

WHAT IS DUKKAH? Dukkah, or duqqa, is a Middle Eastern condiment made of herbs, nuts, and toasted spices. The blend typically contains hazelnuts, cumin, sesame seeds, coriander, salt, and pepper. It is mixed with oil and eaten with bread. Dukkah is thought to have originated in Egypt, with the name meaning "to crush," similar to how the blend is made in a mortar and pestle. Variations are commonly eaten throughout the Middle East. While the main components of dukkah are standard, brands, restaurants, and families have their own unique blends of herbs and spices to make it their own.

FAVA FALAFEL

While many falafel dishes we see today are chickpea based, fava beans are thought to be the traditional ingredient originally used in Egypt. Today, falafel is considered to be one of Israel's national dishes and can be found across the country as a part of main dishes, snacks, and street food.

Baked Herby Falafel Balls

SERVES
4; makes approximately 12 falafel

ON THE TABLE IN...
10 hours 45 minutes, including
at least 10 hours soaking time

Falafel has long been my go-to protein choice, but frying falafel can feel like a chore. In this recipe you don't need a fryer for a delicious falafel, but there is one thing you can't skip: the secret to falafel is using dried chickpeas that have been soaked, not canned or cooked chickpeas, which will result in mushy, lifeless falafel. Soaking beans overnight means that falafel is rarely a spur-of-the-moment dish, though I like to keep a portion of soaked and drained chickpeas in the freezer for when a craving hits. Instead of frying, I bake or air fry my falafel for a less messy, healthier variety that I can add to my salads, mezze platters, or even tacos.

In a bowl, combine the chickpeas and water and soak for at least 10 hours or overnight.

Preheat the oven to 400°F. Line a sheet pan with parchment paper. Use a pastry brush to brush 2 tablespoons of the oil on the parchment paper.

In a food processor or blender, combine the soaked chickpeas, shallot, garlic, sesame seeds, lemon zest, cumin, coriander, salt, red chili flakes, baking powder, parsley, and cilantro and pulse until combined, but not totally smooth.

Use a 1-tablespoon measure to scoop the mixture into 2-tablespoon mounds and shape them into balls using your hands (if it is sticking to your hands, wet them slightly before rolling). Place the balls on the prepared sheet pan.

Brush the falafel balls with the remaining 4 tablespoons of olive oil. Bake for 25 minutes, flipping the balls halfway through, until browned.

1 cup dried chickpeas
2 cups water
6 tablespoons olive oil, divided
1 shallot, peeled and quartered
4 garlic cloves, peeled
2 tablespoons sesame seeds
1 teaspoon lemon zest
1 teaspoon ground cumin
1 teaspoon ground coriander
½ teaspoon salt
¼ teaspoon red chili flakes
¼ teaspoon baking powder
1 cup roughly chopped fresh parsley
1 cup roughly chopped fresh cilantro

NOTE: Uncooked falafel balls can be frozen for up to 1 month. Bake from frozen for 25 to 30 minutes in the oven at 400°F, or until heated through. Reheat cooked falafel in the oven or air fryer at 400°F for 5 to 6 minutes.

VARIATION: Instead of baking, air fry the falafel balls at 375°F for 12 to 15 minutes until crispy.

Hearty Lentil Goulash

SERVES	ON THE TABLE IN...	
6	1 hour	

The Jewish cuisine of my childhood was centered around meat, potatoes, rice, and the occasional mixed green salad with "Italian dressing." Wintertime meals were filled with stews, soups, and one-pot meals bubbling on the stove. One of those was goulash. One of Hungary's national dishes, goulash is a hearty stew that is customarily made with beef, onion, carrots, and potatoes and seasoned with Hungarian paprika. While beef is commonly used, in times of scarcity, beans were often substituted. This version uses lentils in place of beef and is seasoned with umami-rich soy sauce and fragrant caraway for a hearty vegan twist on the classic. Serve it with fried polenta, buttered noodles, rice, or crusty bread.

3 tablespoons extra-virgin olive oil

1 medium yellow onion, chopped

1 yellow potato, cut into ½-inch pieces

2 medium carrots, cut into ¼-inch pieces

1 medium red bell pepper, cut into ½-inch chunks

6 garlic cloves, finely chopped

¼ cup sweet Hungarian paprika

1 cup dried green or brown lentils, rinsed

1½ cups canned diced tomatoes, with liquid

3 cups vegetable broth, low-sodium if preferred

½ cup dry red wine

1½ tablespoons soy sauce, or gluten-free tamari, if preferred

1 bay leaf

¼ teaspoon caraway seeds, crushed

Salt

Pepper

In a large saucepan or Dutch oven, heat the olive oil over medium heat until hot, but not smoking. Add the onion, stir to coat with the oil, and cook until it begins to soften, 6 to 8 minutes.

Add the potato, carrots, bell pepper, garlic, and paprika, stir to combine, and cook for 2 to 3 minutes (this helps the paprika release flavor). Add the lentils, canned tomatoes, vegetable broth, red wine, soy sauce, bay leaf, and caraway seeds and bring to a boil over medium-high heat.

Lower the heat to a simmer, cover, and cook until the lentils are tender, 30 to 35 minutes. If there is still too much liquid, remove the lid and simmer for 5 minutes more. Remove and discard the bay leaf.

Season with salt and pepper to taste.

NOTE: Store the goulash in an airtight container in the fridge for up to 5 days or in the freezer for up to 3 months.

VARIATION: If preferred, omit the caraway seeds.

ALL ABOUT PAPRIKA *Paprika* is the Hungarian word for "pepper," and as one of Hungary's national dishes, goulash wouldn't be the same without it. There are many types of paprika on the market, including hot paprika, smoked paprika, and Hungarian paprika. I tend to stay away from "basic paprika," which is labeled as simply "paprika," and is very mild in flavor, imparting more color than flavor to dishes. Hot paprika is made using spicy peppers, and smoked paprika is a Spanish variety with a rich, earthy, smoky flavor. Hungarian paprika is complex, with a typically sweet flavor that comes from a process of toasting and drying different varieties of peppers. When it comes to paprika, it's been my favorite spice since I was a child. In fact, I wanted to legally change my name to "Paprika" for a number of years (no lie!).

WHAT IS TEMPEH?

High in protein and fiber, tempeh is made of soybeans and typically one or more grains (rice and millet are common) that have been fermented and formed into a beige and white cake. Tempeh has a firm texture that lends itself well to stews and other recipes that would traditionally use ground beef. With an umami-rich flavor profile—think nutty and mushroomy—it adds meaty flavor to recipes like tomato sauce or vegan cholents like this one.

Tempeh and Bean Cholent

SERVES
8 to 10

ON THE TABLE IN...
1 hour 45 minutes

Cholent is a uniquely Jewish dish that was created specifically to be prepared before sundown on Friday and cooked over low heat overnight to be enjoyed warm on Saturday, and cholent has become known as a Sabbath stew. Traditional cholent contains meat, potatoes, barley, and beans, though this vegan version uses hearty tempeh and is flavored with turmeric, orange juice, and rosemary and studded with dates. You can make this in a slow cooker, but it can be ready in just over 1 hour, making it an easy, low-effort dinner for any day of the week.

Preheat the oven to 350°F.

In a large, oven-safe pot or Dutch oven, heat the olive oil over medium heat until it shimmers. Add the tempeh, onion, garlic, and carrots and cook until the tempeh starts to turn golden and the onions begin to soften, 10 to 12 minutes.

Add the paprika and turmeric and stir until evenly coated. Add the sweet potato, vegetable broth, tomatoes, orange juice, barley, dates, kidney beans, white beans, chickpeas, rosemary, bay leaf, and soy sauce and mix until combined.

Cover and bake for 70 to 90 minutes, or until it has thickened and the barley is tender. If there is too much liquid, remove the lid and continue to cook for 5 to 8 minutes, or until the liquid evaporates slightly.

Remove from the oven, remove the bay leaf and rosemary sprig, and stir in the miso. Season with salt and pepper to taste. Serve with the chopped parsley.

NOTE: Leftover cholent can be stored in an airtight container in the fridge for up to 5 days or frozen for up to 3 months.

VARIATIONS: Add a knob of fresh ginger and remove it with the bay leaf and rosemary before serving. To make in a slow cooker, add all the ingredients to the pot. Cook on low for 12 hours.

3 tablespoons extra-virgin olive oil

1 (8-oz) package tempeh, crumbled

1 medium yellow onion, cut into ¼-inch pieces

5 garlic cloves, chopped

4 medium carrots, cut into ¼-inch slices

1 tablespoon smoked paprika

1 teaspoon ground turmeric

1 medium sweet potato, cut into ½-inch pieces

2 cups low-sodium vegetable broth

1 (28-oz) can chopped tomatoes

½ cup orange juice

⅓ cup pearled barley, rinsed

¼ cup pitted chopped dates

1 cup canned red kidney beans, drained and rinsed

1 cup canned white beans, drained and rinsed

1 cup canned chickpeas, drained and rinsed

1 sprig fresh rosemary

1 bay leaf

1 tablespoon soy sauce

1 tablespoon white miso paste

Sea salt

Pepper

½ cup chopped fresh parsley

Olive, Chickpea, and Zucchini Stew with Preserved Lemons

SERVES	ON THE TABLE IN…	
6	1 hour	

This tagine-inspired stew reminds me of my travels in Morocco, where we made our own chickpea and vegetable tagines using produce and spices we purchased at local markets. The sights, smells, and combination of spices was mesmerizing. After visiting the local Marrakech synagogue and learning about the rich history of North African Jewry (Maghrebi Jews), tagine struck me as a great Shabbat meal that honors the Jews of Morocco. Tagine is named for the clay, earthen pot that the stew is cooked in. For accessibility (you probably don't have a tagine hanging around), this dish is cooked in a tall-sided skillet for a new take on Friday-night dinner.

3 tablespoons extra-virgin olive oil

1 medium yellow onion, finely chopped

3 garlic cloves, finely chopped

2 carrots, cut into ¼-inch rounds

4 zucchinis, cut into ½-inch half-moons

2 teaspoons ground cumin

1½ teaspoons ground coriander

1 teaspoon ground turmeric

½ teaspoon ground cinnamon

1 tablespoon sweet paprika

½ teaspoon sea salt

1 (14-oz) can chickpeas, drained and rinsed

2 tablespoons chopped preserved lemon

⅓ cup roughly chopped dried apricots

½ cup pitted green olives

1 cup vegetable broth, low-sodium if preferred

Cooked Israeli (pearl) couscous or basmati rice, for serving, optional

½ cup chopped fresh cilantro, for serving

In a large, tall-sided skillet, heat the olive oil over medium heat. Add the onion and cook, stirring occasionally, until the onion begins to soften, 5 to 6 minutes.

Add the garlic, carrots, and zucchini and cook until they begin to soften, 3 to 4 minutes. Add the cumin, coriander, turmeric, cinnamon, paprika, and salt and mix until evenly distributed. Add the chickpeas, preserved lemon, dried apricots, green olives, and vegetable broth and bring to a boil. Decrease the heat to medium-low and simmer until the broth has thickened slightly, 20 to 25 minutes.

Serve over couscous or rice and top with fresh cilantro.

NOTE: Store this stew in an airtight container for up to 5 days in the fridge or up to 3 months in the freezer.

VARIATION: If you can't find preserved lemons, use 1 tablespoon of lemon zest and 2 teaspoons of lemon juice.

WHAT ARE PRESERVED LEMONS? Originating in Algeria, Tunisia, and Moroccan cuisine, preserved lemons made a splash in North American kitchens in the mid to late twentieth century. I use them in soups, stews, and salad dressings or stirred into hummus or labneh for a zippy dip. It's also good tossed into pasta with olive oil and garlic. Preserved lemons are made by stuffing lemons with salt and letting them ferment. You can find preserved lemons or preserved lemon paste in specialty grocers (and sometimes in grocery store chains).

Sabich Grain Bowl with Crispy Chickpeas

SERVES	ON THE TABLE IN...	
4	1 hour	

This recipe is inspired by one of my favorite Israeli fast foods, the classic sabich pita, and it consists of creamy fried eggplant, hard-boiled eggs, and a healthy portion of tahini, resulting in a grain bowl that satisfies all my cravings. With nutty sesame-studded barley, za'atar baked eggplant and chickpeas, a jammy egg, and salad with pickles, drizzled with a creamy tahini sauce and amba (see page 36), its multiple ingredients naturally lend themselves to choose-your-own-adventure bowls. Add fresh greens, sauerkraut, and chopped vegetables for a do-it-yourself dinner or meal-prep lunch.

GRAINS

1 cup pearl barley, rinsed

3 cups vegetable broth, low-sodium if preferred

1 teaspoon garlic powder

¼ cup sesame seeds

EGGPLANT AND CHICKPEAS

1 medium Italian globe eggplant, cut into ¼-inch slices

1 teaspoon sea salt

1 (14-oz) can chickpeas, drained and rinsed

3 tablespoons extra-virgin olive oil

2 teaspoons za'atar

CHOPPED SALAD

1 cup cherry tomatoes, quartered

⅓ English cucumber, cut into ½-inch pieces

¼ medium red onion, finely chopped

¼ cup chopped fresh parsley

¼ cup (2 or 3) chopped small kosher pickles

1 teaspoon lemon juice

¼ teaspoon sea salt

4 hard-boiled eggs

Make the grains In a medium saucepan, combine the pearl barley, vegetable broth, garlic powder, and sesame seeds and bring to a boil over medium-high heat. Cover, lower the heat to a simmer, and cook until the liquid is absorbed and the grains are chewy, 25 to 30 minutes.

Make the eggplant and chickpeas On a large sheet pan, arrange the sliced eggplant in a single layer. Sprinkle with the salt and let sit for 10 minutes. Dab the eggplant dry using a paper towel. Salting the eggplant will draw out extra moisture, and beads of water will be present. Add the chickpeas, drizzle with the olive oil, and sprinkle with the za'atar. Using your hands, toss to evenly distribute.

Roast the eggplant and chickpea mixture for 20 to 25 minutes, or until the eggplant is tender and the chickpeas are crisp.

Make the chopped salad While the vegetables are roasting, combine the cherry tomatoes, cucumber, red onion, parsley, and pickles in a medium bowl. Toss with the lemon juice, and season with salt. Set aside.

Peel the eggs and cut them in half.

Make the dressing In a small bowl, whisk together the tahini, water, lemon juice, lemon zest, and cumin.

Assemble the bowls Divide the barley among 4 bowls. Top with the eggplant and chickpeas, chopped salad, and halved boiled eggs. Drizzle with the tahini dressing.

NOTE: Store all the components separately in airtight containers in the fridge for up to 5 days.

VARIATION: Use rice, quinoa, or freekeh in place of the barley. For a vegan variation, omit the hard-boiled egg.

DRESSING

¼ cup tahini

3 tablespoons water

1 tablespoon lemon juice

1 teaspoon lemon zest

Pinch ground cumin

WHAT IS SABICH?

Sabich is a pita or laffa sandwich of fried eggplant, boiled eggs, tomato and cucumber salad, parsley, tahini, and amba sauce, which is popular in Israel. Brought to Israel via Iraqi Jews, sabich relies on precooked and premade eggplant, eggs, and salad for an easy breakfast or Shabbat meal.

WHAT IS CELERIAC? A much underrated vegetable, celeriac, also known as celery root, is the root of a celery plant and looks like a bumpy, round potato. It has a sweet, earthy flavor with a hint of celery. Texturally, it is a cross between a turnip and a potato. They often have dirt stuck in the skin, so be sure to give it a good scrub. Peel them if the recipe instructs. I like to cube and roast celeriac, use it as a mashed potato alternative, shave it raw into salads, or blend it into a soup.

Celeriac "Pastrami" Sandwich

SERVES	ON THE TABLE IN...
4 to 6	6 hours, including at least 2 hours of marinating

As a kid, I remember going to Jewish delis with my dad and zaida, and I would be mesmerized by the towering stack of pastrami and corned beef in the sandwiches. They were so big that even the grown-ups would share a sandwich, and we'd have leftovers to take home and fry with eggs the next morning. I stopped eating pastrami long before I stopped eating meat, but that doesn't mean I never craved it. Instead of meat, celeriac is the star in this recipe. It is slow roasted, marinated in a beet-red mixture that mimics the flavor and appearance of pastrami, and baked for a satisfying replacement of the deli classic.

Preheat the oven to 325°F.

Make the celeriac "pastrami" Scrub the celeriac well to remove any dirt. Place in a 9-by-13-inch baking dish. Drizzle with the olive oil and season with the salt and pepper. Roast for 2½ hours or until fork-tender. Let cool.

Make the marinade In a blender, combine the beet, liquid smoke, soy sauce, maple syrup, Dijon mustard, salt, onion powder, garlic powder, black pepper, coriander, allspice, water, and olive oil and blend until smooth.

Cut the celeriac into ⅛-inch slices. Return to the baking dish. Pour the marinade over the celeriac, put in the refrigerator, and let sit for at least 2 hours or up to 24 hours.

Increase the oven temperature to 350°F.

continued

CELERIAC "PASTRAMI"

2 whole celeriac

3 tablespoons olive oil

1 teaspoon sea salt

½ teaspoon black pepper

MARINADE

1 medium beet

2 tablespoons liquid smoke

2 tablespoons soy sauce, or gluten-free tamari, if preferred

1 tablespoon maple syrup

2 teaspoons Dijon mustard

1 teaspoon sea salt

1 teaspoon onion powder

1 teaspoon garlic powder

1 teaspoon black pepper

1 teaspoon ground coriander

¼ teaspoon ground allspice

½ cup water

3 tablespoons olive oil

continued

SEASONING

1 teaspoons black pepper

½ teaspoon ground coriander

½ teaspoon sea salt

TO ASSEMBLE EACH SANDWICH

2 slices rye bread, gluten-free if preferred

1 tablespoon Russian dressing

2 tablespoons sauerkraut

2 slices white cheese or vegan alternative

Olive oil, for cooking

Use the seasoning After marinating, sprinkle the celeriac with the pepper, coriander, and salt and bake for 30 minutes.

Assemble each sandwich Pile the celeriac onto a slice of rye bread, slather it with Russian dressing, and top with sauerkraut and cheese. Finish with another slice of rye bread. Repeat for however many sandwiches you are making.

Heat the oil in a skillet over medium heat, add a sandwich, and cook until crispy and heated through, 4 to 5 minutes per side.

NOTE: This recipe takes time. To make it easier, split the tasks into sections. On one day, roast the celeriac and marinate. The following day, bake the slices and make the sandwich. Prepared slices of celeriac will last for up to 5 days in an airtight container in the refrigerator. Assemble the sandwich just before serving.

VARIATION: Add the celeriac to a wrap, quesadilla, or your favorite sandwich. Use vegan cheese, if preferred.

Sweet and Spicy Harissa Hasselback Squash with Chickpeas

ON THE TABLE IN...
1 hour 30 minutes

I'm constantly looking for vegetable-focused recipes that don't need to pretend to be something else, that everyone will love, and that can be the centerpiece of any holiday meal. Many people are intimidated by squash, wondering how to peel it, prepare it, and what to make with it. Luckily, most squash skin is edible, butternut squash included, meaning you can save a step (and headache) by leaving it unpeeled. The combination of sweet butternut squash and spicy, smoky harissa is balanced out with tart lemon juice, for an appealingly sweet and sour dish. The secret to this recipe is date syrup, or silan, a sweet, molasses-like complex flavor that tastes less sweet than honey or agave.

Preheat the oven to 400°F.

Halve the squash lengthwise. Use a spoon to scoop out the seeds. Rub the skin of the squash with oil. Place the squash, flesh side down, in a 9-by-13-inch baking dish and roast for 20 minutes, or until it begins to soften slightly. If using a smaller honeynut squash, you can skip this step.

Meanwhile, combine the harissa powder, 3 tablespoons olive oil, date syrup, 2 tablespoons of the lemon juice, and salt in a small bowl and mix well.

Remove the squash from the oven. Place the squash cut side down on a cutting board.

Using a sharp knife, cut through the skin side of the squash crosswise, being careful not to cut all the way through. Continue to cut the rest of the squash into ⅛-inch slices. Try putting chopsticks or wooden spoon handles on either side of the squash to prevent cutting through.

continued

1 medium (about 1½ lb) unpeeled butternut squash

3 tablespoons extra-virgin olive oil, plus more as needed

2 tablespoons harissa powder

¼ cup date syrup

4 tablespoons lemon juice, divided

¼ teaspoon sea salt

1 (14-oz) can chickpeas, drained and rinsed

⅓ cup feta cheese, crumbled

¼ cup chopped pumpkin seeds

½ cup chopped fresh parsley

Return the squash to the baking dish, scored side up. Add the chickpeas to the baking dish. Use a pastry brush to brush the oil mixture over the top of the squash, allowing it to get into each slice. Reserve the remaining mixture.

Bake for 30 to 40 minutes, or until softened, spooning any excess syrup mixture over the chickpeas halfway through.

Top with crumbled feta (if using), pumpkin seeds, parsley, and the remaining 2 tablespoons of lemon juice.

NOTE: This dish can also be served at room temperature. Make it 2 hours in advance. Store leftovers in an airtight container in the refrigerator for up to 4 days.

VARIATION: Use sweet potatoes or honeynut squash in place of butternut to create a single-serving side dish. Omit the feta if vegan, and sprinkle with hemp seeds or vegan feta cheese. If you can't find date syrup, use maple syrup instead.

WHAT IS HARISSA?

This North African spice blend or paste is made primarily of hot chili peppers. It is commonly used in vegetable dishes and stews, and lends a smoky, spicy flavor to dishes. While harissa varies from region to region, it nearly always contains red pepper, chili pepper, and a variety of spices or even rose petals.

SHAKSHUKA This is a popular breakfast or brunch dish with origins in North Africa (Tunisia, Algeria, Libya, Morocco). Spicy stewed tomato sauce filled with garlic, peppers, cumin, and paprika acts as a poaching liquid for runny eggs. *Shakshuka* means "a mixture" or "shaken up" in Tunisian dialect. Shakshuka was brought to Israel via North African Jewish immigrants in the mid-1900s and has more recently made its way onto North American brunch menus.

Chickpea and Olive Shakshuka

SERVES
4

ON THE TABLE IN...
45 minutes

Shakshuka has long been my default midweek meal. Whether serving brunch for a crowd, a busy weeknight dinner, or an easy pantry meal, shakshuka is one of my favorite dishes to make because it is made in one pan and is endlessly customizable (I like adding vegetables that are on their last legs!). Instead of eggs, this recipe uses chickpeas for easy plant-based protein straight from the pantry. I use harissa seasoning for added depth of flavor and heat, along with umami-rich nutritional yeast and salty green olives to make a hearty dish ideal for anything from breakfast to dinner. A healthy drizzle of tahini before serving gives this vegan dish a richness that the egg yolks would have otherwise offered. Serve with grilled challah, pita, or even spooned over a bowl of rice for a weeknight meal.

In a 9-inch skillet, heat the oil over medium heat until it shimmers. Add the onion, garlic, and bell pepper and sauté until they begin to soften, 5 minutes.

Add the smoked paprika, cumin, and harissa powder, stir until evenly distributed, and cook for 5 to 7 minutes.

Add the canned tomatoes, vegetable broth, and nutritional yeast and bring to a low boil. Decrease the heat to medium-low and simmer for 15 minutes.

Stir in the chickpeas and green olives and simmer until the tomato sauce has thickened slightly, an additional 15 to 20 minutes. Season with salt and pepper to taste.

To serve, drizzle the shakshuka with the tahini and sprinkle with the sesame seeds and parsley.

NOTE: Store leftover shakshuka in an airtight container in the refrigerator for up to 5 days or freeze for up to 3 months.

VARIATION: If you can't find harissa powder, use ¼ teaspoon red chili flakes instead. If you do eat eggs, add them with 5 minutes to spare to make an extra-hearty dish.

2 tablespoons extra-virgin olive oil

1 medium yellow onion, finely chopped

3 garlic cloves, finely chopped

1 medium red bell pepper, cored and cut into ½-inch pieces

1½ teaspoons smoked paprika

1 teaspoon ground cumin

1 teaspoon harissa powder

1 (15-oz) can diced tomatoes

¾ cup low-sodium vegetable broth

1 tablespoon nutritional yeast

1 (14-oz) can chickpeas, drained and rinsed

¼ cup pitted sliced green olives

Salt

Black pepper

3 tablespoons tahini

2 teaspoons sesame seeds

¼ cup chopped fresh parsley

Za'atar and Feta Khachapuri

MAKES	ON THE TABLE IN…			
6 personal-size khachapuri	3 hours, including 1 hour 15 minutes resting time			

Strolling through the markets of Jerusalem, it is hard not to run into someone rolling, folding, and baking a hot khachapuri. Brought to Israel via Georgian Jews, it has become a part of Israeli cuisine. To me, khachapuri reminds me of snacking my way through Israeli markets and sitting down for a hearty meal to fuel a day of exploring. These personal-size khachapuri are seasoned with a sesame-studded crust and a generous helping of za'atar and are fun to serve any time of the day. For an interactive dinner, have guests fill their own with optional additions like spinach, roasted peppers, sliced olives, or roasted vegetables. I've included two versions here: one is vegan and one contains egg and dairy.

DOUGH

1 tablespoon olive oil, plus more as needed

1 tablespoon sugar

1 teaspoon sea salt

2¼ teaspoons (7g envelope) instant yeast

2 cups bread flour

¾ cup milk, warmed

NON-VEGAN FILLING

¾ cup crumbled feta cheese

1½ cups whole milk ricotta cheese

2 teaspoons lemon zest

3 tablespoons za'atar

6 large egg yolks

VEGAN FILLING

1 (14-oz) block extra-firm tofu

1 tablespoon lemon juice

2 teaspoons lemon zest

2 garlic cloves, minced

2 tablespoons nutritional yeast

1 tablespoon miso paste

3 tablespoons tahini

2 tablespoons za'atar

½ teaspoon sea salt

Make the dough Grease a medium bowl with oil. Set aside.

Combine the sugar, salt, yeast, and bread flour in the bowl of a stand mixer or a large bowl. Mix to combine.

Attach the dough hook to the stand mixer, add the milk, and mix on medium-low for 2 to 3 minutes, or until a dough begins to form. Add the 1 tablespoon of oil and mix on medium speed for 6 to 8 minutes, or until a soft dough forms.

If using a large bowl, combine the sugar, salt, yeast, and bread flour, and stir until well combined. Add the milk and oil, and mix with a wooden spoon until a rough dough forms. Turn the dough out onto a floured work surface and knead until a soft dough forms, 8 to 10 minutes.

Transfer the dough to the greased bowl. Cover and let rise in a warm place for 1 hour, or until doubled in size.

Make the filling

Non-vegan: In a medium bowl, mix the feta cheese, ricotta, lemon zest, and za'atar using a fork.

Vegan: In a medium bowl, mash the tofu using a fork. Add the lemon juice, lemon zest, garlic, nutritional yeast, miso paste, tahini, za'atar, and salt and mix until combined.

Preheat the oven to 375°F. Line 2 sheet pans with parchment paper.

Punch down the dough to decrease air in the dough. Transfer the dough to a lightly floured surface. Divide the dough into 6 pieces, slightly smaller than a tennis ball. Roll each piece of dough into a ball. Cover the dough balls with a clean kitchen towel. Keep the dough covered while working with each ball.

Using a rolling pin, roll each ball into a 9-inch oval, approximately ¼ inch thick. Use both hands to roll both sides of one of the ovals toward the center, pinching at the top and bottom to make a boat shape. Transfer the shaped dough to the prepared sheet pan and repeat with the remaining dough. You can freeze the shaped dough and fill when frozen, letting them rise 30 minutes before baking. Freeze on the sheet pan in a single layer.

Fill each khachapuri with ¼ to ⅓ cup of filling. Cover and let rest for 15 to 20 minutes.

Make the egg wash

Non-vegan: Whisk together the egg and water. Use a pastry brush to brush the mixture on the border of the boat. Sprinkle it with the sesame seeds and za'atar.

Vegan: Whisk together the maple syrup and water. Use a pastry brush to brush the mixture on the border of the boat and sprinkle with the sesame seeds and za'atar.

Bake for 10 to 15 minutes or until they begin to brown. Place an egg yolk (non-vegan filling) in the center of each boat and bake for an additional 4 to 5 minutes, or until cooked through.

NON-VEGAN EGG WASH

1 egg white
1 tablespoon water
3 tablespoons sesame seeds
2 tablespoons za'atar

VEGAN WASH

1 tablespoon maple syrup
1 tablespoon water
3 tablespoons sesame seeds
2 tablespoons za'atar

NOTE: To make ahead, prepare the dough the night before and let it rise in the fridge. Khachapuri is best the day it is made, but if there are leftovers, refrain from adding the egg until just before serving. Add the egg to the khachapuri and reheat it until the egg is cooked.

SUBSTITUTION: Substitute premade pizza dough for the base if you are short on time.

WHAT IS KHACHAPURI? The national dish of Georgia, khachapuri is a cheese-filled bread. A yeasted bread dough is molded into an oblong boat shape, filled with cheese, and topped with an egg yolk. Baked until golden and the yolk is *just* cooked, it is eaten by tearing off the bread and dipping it into the runny yolk and cheese.

Confit Tomato, Garlic, and White Beans with Zhoug

SERVES	ON THE TABLE IN...	
6	1 hour 45 minutes	

When tomato season rolls around, there is nothing better than slicing into a ripe and juicy tomato—but for the other ten months of the year, tomatoes often leave a lot to be desired. Low and slow roasting brings out the natural sugars in tomatoes, concentrating their flavor until jammy. Paired with spicy, herbaceous zhoug and savory sunflower seeds, this rich dish is a great cold-weather main.

CONFIT
12 ounces grape or cherry tomatoes

8 garlic cloves, peeled

2 (14-oz) cans white beans, drained and rinsed

1 cup extra-virgin olive oil

2 tablespoons lemon zest

½ teaspoon salt

½ teaspoon pepper

TAMARI SUNFLOWER SEEDS
½ cup sunflower seeds

2 tablespoons soy sauce, or gluten-free tamari, if preferred

⅓ cup Zhoug (page 239)

TO SERVE
Pita or toasted challah (optional)

Preheat the oven to 300°F.

Make the confit In an 8-by-8-inch baking dish, combine the tomatoes, garlic, white beans, olive oil, lemon zest, salt, and pepper and mix well. Bake for 1½ hours, or until the tomatoes have blistered and softened completely.

Make the tamari sunflower seeds Line a sheet pan with aluminum foil. In a small bowl, combine the sunflower seeds and tamari and toss to combine. Transfer the mixture to the prepared sheet pan and spread them out in a single layer. Bake for 9 to 11 minutes, or until roasted, checking every 2 to 3 minutes to ensure they don't burn. Let cool.

To serve, spoon the tomato mixture into bowls and top with the zhoug and sunflower seeds. Serve with pita or toasted challah, if desired.

NOTE: Save the confit in the fridge for up to 2 weeks and use in salad dressings or as a finishing oil over pasta, vegetable dishes, or dips.

VARIATION: Omit the pita and serve this over Creamy Mamaliga (page 107) for a comforting wintery dish.

WHAT IS CONFIT? Confit is a French technique of preservation. Food is slowly cooked at a low temperature in oil or sugar syrup. The main thing you need is time and fat, and in this case it's olive oil. Slow cooking helps make any dish tender and can be used on meats, vegetables, and even fruits. While most confit dishes are cooked between 200°F and 250°F for over 3 hours, this dish achieves the same taste and texture in half the time.

Baking & Desserts

Kitchen Sink Mandelbrot

MAKES
2 dozen

ON THE TABLE IN...
2 hours 15 minutes, including
1 hour 10 minutes resting time

My bubbe Muriel was known for a few signature dishes: a breakfast casserole, lemon bars, and her komishbrot, or mandelbrot. She would make two variations that had a tendency to disappear because everyone loved them so much. One was made with candied cherries and chocolate chips, and the other with chocolate sprinkles and hazelnuts. Her recipes were used to fill the dessert table during my wedding. The recipe here pays homage to her delicious crunchy cookies.

⅔ cup water

3 tablespoons ground flax seeds

⅔ cup neutral oil, such as
   avocado or grapeseed

⅔ cup sugar

1 teaspoon sea salt

2 teaspoons vanilla extract

2 cups all-purpose flour

1½ teaspoons baking powder

1½ teaspoons instant
   ground coffee

1 teaspoon ground cinnamon

½ cup pretzels, finely chopped

½ cup salted potato chips,
   crushed

½ cup mini chocolate chips

½ cup unsalted peanuts, chopped

¼ cup shredded unsweetened
   coconut

1 teaspoon flaky sea salt

NOTE: Mandelbrot can be stored in the freezer for up to 6 months in an airtight container. Prepare the dough up to 2 days in advance and store, wrapped in plastic, in the refrigerator.

Line a large sheet pan with parchment paper.

In a small bowl, combine the water and ground flax seeds and mix well to make a flax egg. Let sit for 5 minutes, until thickened.

In the bowl of a stand mixer, or in a large bowl, mix the oil, sugar, and salt. Add the flax egg and vanilla and mix until well combined. Add the flour, baking powder, ground coffee, and cinnamon and mix on low speed until just combined. Add the pretzels, potato chips, chocolate chips, peanuts, and coconut and mix on low until evenly distributed.

Wrap the dough in plastic wrap and refrigerate for at least 1 hour or up to 3 days.

Preheat the oven to 350°F.

Shape the dough into 4 logs, about 1½ to 2 inches wide and 5 inches long, on the sheet pan. Sprinkle with the flaky salt. Bake for 25 to 30 minutes, or until they are firm and slightly puffed.

Let cool on a wire rack for 10 minutes. Lower the oven temperature to 300°F.

Using a sharp knife, cut the cooled logs into ¾-inch-wide slices (7 to 10 per log). Place the slices back on the sheet pan on their sides. Bake for about 25 minutes, or until crisp, flipping halfway through.

Let cool slightly before serving.

Mohn (Poppy Seed) Cookies

MAKES
24 cookies

ON THE TABLE IN...
45 minutes

Poppy seed desserts are a favorite in my family. My dad seeks out poppy seed rolls on every family holiday, road trip, or pit stop. Beyond the rolls, my great-grandmother Sara was known for her poppy seed cookies, called mohn cookies. Slightly cakey and packed with vanilla, they were the perfect afternoon snack. I prefer mine just baked with a touch of golden color on the edges, whereas my grandfather preferred his to be nearly burnt (why, I'll never know).

Preheat the oven to 350°F. Line 2 sheet pans with parchment paper.

In the bowl of a stand mixer, cream the butter until fluffy, or use a hand mixer to cream for 2 to 3 minutes. Add the sugar, coconut yogurt, vanilla, vinegar, and lemon zest and mix until smooth. Add the flour, cornstarch, baking powder, baking soda, and salt and mix until just combined. Add the poppy seeds and mix to incorporate.

On a floured surface, roll out the dough to ¼ inch thickness. Using a 2½- to 3-inch cookie cutter or a glass, cut circles out of the dough. Reroll the scraps and repeat until no dough remains. Optional: Brush any excess flour off the cookies.

Transfer the cookies to the sheet pans. Bake for 10 to 12 minutes, or until puffy and slightly golden on the bottom.

Let cool on the pan for 10 minutes, and then transfer to a wire rack.

¼ cup unsalted vegan butter, at room temperature

½ cup sugar

½ cup coconut yogurt or vegan sour cream

4 teaspoons vanilla extract

¼ teaspoon white vinegar

½ teaspoon lemon zest

1½ cups all-purpose flour, plus more as needed

1 tablespoon cornstarch

1½ tablespoons baking powder

¼ teaspoon baking soda

¼ teaspoon sea salt

2 tablespoons poppy seeds

BAKING & DESSERTS

NOTE: Bake these cookies to your preference, whether you like them pale and soft or golden and crisp—there is no wrong way to enjoy mohn cookies.

VARIATION: Frost these with a powdered sugar frosting, using the recipe from Passover Black and White Cookies (page 180).

SUBSTITUTION: If you eat dairy, use dairy versions of the butter and yogurt.

POPPY SEEDS

Eastern European baked goods are often studded with nutty-flavored poppy seeds. Typically used as a sweet filling, they may also be added to dressings, baked into bread, or sprinkled on top of pastries. Poppy seeds (*mohn* in Yiddish and German) are a favorite ingredient in my kitchen; they are delicious, and they also symbolize a bright future.

Passover Black and White Cookies

MAKES
8 cookies

ON THE TABLE IN...
2 hours 30 minutes,
including 1 hour of resting time

A New York deli staple, black and white cookies hold a special place in our household. My late father-in-law was "a kid from the Bronx," and he raised my husband to appreciate deli classics, especially black and white cookies. The connection to his father, his childhood, and his memory lives on in the food memories they shared together. I have been searching for a sweet, soft, lemon-scented cookie topped with a layer of chocolate and vanilla frosting. I wanted a Passover dessert that I would crave all year-round, and these cookies are just that. It is a vegan, gluten-free, and Passover-friendly recipe that I think rivals your deli favorite. If serving these during Passover, check to make sure your ingredients are Passover-friendly.

COOKIES
1½ cups almond flour, sifted
¼ cup arrowroot starch
1 teaspoon baking powder
¼ teaspoon sea salt
1 tablespoon melted coconut oil
¼ cup maple syrup
1 teaspoon vanilla extract
½ teaspoon lemon zest
1½ teaspoons lemon juice

FROSTING
1½ cups powdered sugar
½ teaspoon vanilla extract
2 teaspoons lemon juice
1 to 2 tablespoons water
1 tablespoons light agave syrup
  or corn syrup
2 to 3 tablespoons cocoa powder

Make the cookies In a medium bowl, whisk together the almond flour, arrowroot starch, baking powder, and salt. Add the coconut oil, maple syrup, vanilla, lemon zest, and lemon juice and mix well until combined. Cover with plastic wrap and refrigerate for at least 30 minutes or up to overnight.

Meanwhile, preheat th e oven to 350°F. Line a large sheet pan with parchment paper.

Divide the dough into 8 equal pieces and roll them into balls. Transfer the balls to the prepared sheet pan and press each one into ½-inch-thick circles. Note: The cookies will not spread.

Bake for 11 to 13 minutes, or until just golden. Let cool on the sheet pan for at least 20 minutes, or until fully cool. Icing warm cookies will make them appear messy, and the icing will not set.

Make the frosting In a medium bowl, combine the powdered sugar, vanilla, lemon juice, and water, 1 tablespoon at a time, whisking to combine. The frosting should be quite thick and run off the spoon in thick ribbons, holding its shape for 2 to 3 seconds before settling back into the bowl. Whisk in the agave.

Divide the frosting equally between 2 bowls. To one bowl, add the cocoa powder. If it looks too thick, add an additional 1 to 2 teaspoons of water.

Using an offset spatula, spread the vanilla frosting on one half of the bottom (flat) side of the cookie. Place the cookie on a clean sheet pan. Repeat with the rest of the cookies, place in the refrigerator, and let rest for 20 minutes, until the frosting is set.

Spread the chocolate frosting on the other side of the cookies and return them to the refrigerator to set, about 20 minutes.

NOTE: Store for up to two weeks in an airtight container in the fridge, or 3 weeks in the freezer. Layer the cookies with wax paper to prevent sticking during storage.

Passover Coconut Macaroons

MAKES	ON THE TABLE IN...	
12 macaroons	45 minutes, including 10 minutes resting time	

Nothing screams Passover like coconut desserts. As a kid, Passover meant toasted coconut marshmallows to me, but it didn't stop there; coconut has long been a family favorite, too, with memories of coconut-laced desserts, including cake, pie, and macaroons, at nearly every celebration. Classic Passover desserts are packed with eggs, but I wanted to share a vegan alternative, without compromising flavor. These macaroons are held together with a mixture of potato starch, coconut milk, and sugar, which caramelizes slightly when baked, and the flavor is balanced with zesty lime and bittersweet chocolate.

2 cups unsweetened shredded coconut

½ cup sugar

⅓ cup potato starch

½ cup canned full-fat coconut milk

1 tablespoon lime juice

½ teaspoon lime zest

¼ teaspoon sea salt

6 ounces (about 1 cup) dark chocolate chips

1 tablespoon coconut oil

Preheat the oven to 325°F. Line a sheet pan with parchment paper.

In a medium bowl, combine the coconut, sugar, potato starch, coconut milk, lime juice, lime zest, and salt until well combined.

Using a cookie scoop or ice cream scoop (large enough to fit approximately 2 tablespoons), scoop up some of the coconut mixture and pack it very firmly into the scoop. Use your fingers or the back of a spoon to press it into the scoop. Gently remove the coconut mound from the scoop and place it onto the prepared sheet pan. Tap the back of the cookie scoop to release it, if needed, and reform the mounds after placing them on the pan. Repeat with the remaining coconut mixture.

Bake for 22 to 25 minutes, or until golden. Let cool on the sheet pan. Once cool, remove them from the pan and place them on a plate. Line the sheet pan with wax paper.

While the macaroons are cooling, combine the chocolate chips and coconut oil in a microwave-safe bowl and microwave in 30-second increments, mixing well between each increment, until smooth.

Once the macaroons are cooled, dip the bottoms into the melted chocolate and place them on the prepared sheet pan. Refrigerate the macaroons until the chocolate is set, about 10 minutes.

NOTE: Once the chocolate has set, store the macaroons in an airtight container at room temperature for up to 5 days or in the refrigerator for up to 2 weeks. Store them in the freezer for up to 3 months.

VARIATION: Add 1 teaspoon of vanilla extract or ¼ teaspoon of almond extract to the mixture in place of the lime zest and lime juice. Fold in 2 tablespoons of rainbow sprinkles and dip them into melted white chocolate.

MACAROONS VS. MACARONS

Macaroons and macarons are *not* the same, despite both being flourless desserts. The added *o* in the word *macaroons* sets them apart from the French delicacy and identifies them as a Passover staple. Macaroons are a flourless cookie made of shredded coconut, egg whites, and sugar and couldn't be simpler to make, whereas macarons are made with finely ground almonds, sandwiched with a sweet filling and tinted with food coloring and are much more complex to make.

Funfetti Hamantaschen

MAKES	ON THE TABLE IN…	
30 to 36	3 hours, including 1 hour of resting time	

Although hamantaschen have always been one of my favorite Jewish treats, they are long overdue for a rebrand from their reputation as a dry, flavorless cookie at the back of the deli case. Every spring, my family would fill, fold, and bake dozens of hamantaschen, filled with poppy seed or prune filling in preparation for Purim. The recipe here is not the prune-filled hamantaschen of my childhood. Inspired by my own springtime birthday, I updated and veganized my favorite holiday cookie with a dash of almond extract, colorful sprinkles, and a simple cashew "cheesecake" filling for a birthday-worthy hamantaschen that can be made all year-round.

DOUGH

¾ cup unsalted vegan butter, at room temperature

½ cup sugar

¼ cup applesauce

1 teaspoon vanilla extract

1 teaspoon almond extract

2¼ cups all-purpose flour, plus more as needed

1 tablespoon cornstarch

1 teaspoon baking powder

¼ teaspoon sea salt

¼ cup rainbow sprinkles

FILLING

1½ cups raw cashews, soaked in hot water for 20 minutes

2 tablespoons cornstarch

2 tablespoons coconut oil, melted

⅓ cup water

¼ cup sugar

1 teaspoons vanilla extract

1 tablespoon lemon juice

1 teaspoon lemon zest

½ teaspoon almond extract

½ teaspoon salt

Make the dough

Food processor: In the bowl of a food processor, combine the vegan butter, sugar, applesauce, vanilla, almond extract, flour, cornstarch, baking powder, and salt, pulsing until just combined. Add the sprinkles, pulsing two or three times to incorporate. The dough should be moist but not sticky.

Stand mixer: Using the paddle attachment, mix the vegan butter, sugar, applesauce, vanilla, and almond extract until light in color. Add the flour, cornstarch, baking powder, and salt and mix on low until just incorporated. Add the sprinkles and mix on low for 1 minute more to evenly distribute.

Flatten the dough into a disk and wrap in plastic wrap. Refrigerate for at least 45 minutes.

Make the filling Drain the cashews. In a high-speed blender or food processor, combine the cashews, cornstarch, melted coconut oil, water, sugar, vanilla, lemon juice, lemon zest, almond extract, and salt and blend until smooth. Note: The mixture will be thick, so you may have to scrape down the sides occasionally to blend. Set aside.

continued

continued

GLAZE

¼ cup plain unsweetened non-dairy milk

2 tablespoons maple syrup

Line 2 sheet pans with parchment paper.

Remove the dough from the fridge and cut it in half. Rewrap one half of the dough with plastic wrap and keep in the fridge. Roll one half of the dough on a well-floured surface to ⅛ inch thickness.

Using a 3-inch circular cookie cutter (or a glass), cut out circles of dough and transfer them to the prepared sheet pans. Reroll the scraps until all the dough is used. If you find the dough is sticking to the cutter, dip it in flour before cutting.

Place 1 teaspoon of the filling in the center of each circle. Pinch the dough into a triangle or fold the left edge of the dough toward the center, covering a small portion of the filling, then fold the right edge of the dough toward the center, slightly overlapping the left, creating a triangle shape, with the point closest to you. Fold over the top of the dough and pinch the edges together, or tuck it over like an envelope. Pinch each corner to secure.

Make the glaze In a small bowl, combine the non-dairy milk and maple syrup. Use a brush to brush the glaze over all the hamantaschen. Transfer the pans to the refrigerator and chill for at least 15 minutes. This will prevent them from opening and losing their shape when baking.

Meanwhile, preheat the oven to 350°F.

Transfer the sheet pans to the oven and bake for 12 to 14 minutes, or until just golden. Note: If you roll the hamantaschen out too thick, it will take longer to bake. Check the hamantaschen for doneness around 12 minutes.

WHAT IS PURIM?

Purim is so much more than hamantaschen. In essence, it is a story about survival. While we typically see hamantaschen during Purim celebrations to mock Haman's (the bad guy) three-pointed hat, they also commemorate saving the Jewish people of Persia from death, as told in the book of Esther. Purim can be celebrated with "hidden" foods, like kreplach or dumplings. With Queen Esther as the star of this joyous holiday, we celebrate her vegetarianism and enjoy bean-based dishes. During Purim, it is customary to give loved ones and those in need *mishloah manot*, or gifts, such as food or kits for those experiencing homelessness.

NOTE: Freeze the hamantaschen in airtight containers for up to 6 months. Prepare the dough and filling up to 4 days in advance and store in airtight containers separately in the refrigerator. Leftover filling is great on top of oatmeal, added to smoothies, or on toast.

VARIATION: To use this hamantaschen dough as a base for other fillings, omit the almond extract and sprinkles. Use a thick filling that won't seep liquid when cooking, such as high-sugar jams (I use Bonne Maman brand), chocolate hazelnut spread, apple butter, or a poppy seed filling. Hamantaschen are a blank canvas for fillings!

Mini Halvah Cakes

MAKES
24 mini cakes

ON THE TABLE IN...
2 hours 15 minutes,
including 2 hours of resting time

Exploring the markets of Israel, you can't help being drawn to the stacks of halvah cakes, topped with everything from pistachios to coffee beans. Halvah is a sweet confection made of ground nuts or seeds (often sesame seeds) and sugar, pressed into a pan and chilled until set. While the larger-than-life cakes of halvah at the market are a treat, the bite-size confections here are great for customizing to your flavor preferences.

Generously grease a mini muffin tin with cooking spray. Add mini muffin paper liners, if desired. Alternatively, grease a loaf pan and line it with parchment paper, leaving some paper hanging over the sides for easy removal. Sprinkle your desired topping into the muffin cups. Set aside.

In a small saucepan, combine the sugar and water and bring to a boil over medium-high heat. Cook until a candy or digital thermometer reaches 245°F to 250°F, or the firm ball stage, 7 to 8 minutes. If you don't have a thermometer, test by dropping a small quantity of syrup into cold water. It should form a firm ball.

Meanwhile, combine the tahini, vanilla, and salt in a heatproof bowl.

Once the sugar reaches 250°F, slowly drizzle the sugar syrup into the bowl with the tahini mixture, stirring constantly with a wooden spoon, and then beating vigorously until smooth and glossy and it pulls away from the sides of the bowl, 2 to 3 minutes. Note: Overmixing your halvah will result in a crumbly texture.

Immediately scoop up the tahini mixture and press it into the muffin cups. Use a spatula to press the mixture down and scrape off the excess to create a smooth layer.

Cover loosely with plastic wrap and refrigerate for a minimum of 2 hours or overnight.

To remove, invert the muffin tin and tap the bottom with a wooden spoon to release the halvah.

⅓ cup topping, such as cacao nibs, chopped pistachios, rose petals, or sprinkles

1¼ cups sugar

⅓ cup + 1 tablespoon water

1¼ cups tahini

1 tablespoon vanilla extract

¼ teaspoon sea salt

NOTE: This recipe will have a chewier, fudgier texture that is more similar to the Eastern European version of halvah, which is usually made with sunflower seeds. This recipe requires a candy thermometer in order for the sugar to reach just the right temperature. Halvah will keep, wrapped in plastic, in the refrigerator for up to 3 months.

Salted Chocolate Rugelach

MAKES
4 dozen

ON THE TABLE IN...
3 hours, including 1 hour 45 minutes
of resting time

Walking through the Mahane Yehuda Market in Jerusalem is not complete without a stop (or two) at Marzipan Bakery, known for their yeasted, syrup-drenched rugelach that melts in your mouth. I grew up in North America, which means that I enjoyed a different type of rugelach, often a cream cheese–based dough, rolled into crescents around a chocolate, nutty cinnamon, or fruit filling and served at every Kiddush luncheon. Inspired by North American hamantaschen and the flavors of Jerusalem's markets, this recipe is slightly nutty thanks to tahini in the dough and has a salted chocolate filling, for an updated flavor profile that is just sweet enough.

DOUGH

1 cup vegan cream cheese

¼ cup vegan butter, at room temperature

3 tablespoons tahini

1 teaspoon vanilla extract

¼ cup powdered sugar

2 cups all-purpose flour, plus more as needed

½ teaspoon baking powder

½ teaspoon salt

FILLING

¼ cup vegan butter, melted

3 tablespoons cocoa powder

¼ cup brown sugar

½ teaspoon espresso powder

1 cup grated dark chocolate, divided

1 teaspoon sea salt, divided

WASH

¼ cup plain unsweetened non-dairy milk

1 tablespoon maple syrup

Flaky sea salt

Make the dough In the bowl of a stand mixer or in a medium bowl, cream the vegan cream cheese, vegan butter, and tahini until light in color. Add the vanilla and powdered sugar and mix on medium speed until combined.

Add the flour, baking powder, and salt and mix on low until just combined. Add 1 to 2 tablespoons of cold water if the dough isn't coming together. The dough should be somewhat sandy, with pebble-size pieces.

Place 4 pieces of plastic wrap on the counter. Place the dough on one of the pieces and form into a ball. Cut the dough into 4 equal pieces. Wrap each piece individually in one of the pieces of plastic wrap. Flatten the balls into disks and refrigerate for 1 hour, or up to overnight.

Line 2 sheet pans with parchment paper.

Make the filling While the dough is chilling, in a small saucepan over medium heat, combine the vegan butter, cocoa powder, brown sugar, espresso powder, ½ cup of the chocolate, and ¼ teaspoon of the salt and stir until melted. Set aside to cool.

Assemble the rugelach On a well-floured surface, roll out each ball of dough into a 9-inch circle, slightly less than ¼ inch thick. I use a cake pan as a guide and cut around the edges with a paring knife. Save the scraps to reroll. Spread 2 tablespoons of the cocoa mixture on one of the circles, all the way to the edges, using an offset spatula. Sprinkle with 2 tablespoons of the remaining ½ cup of grated chocolate and ¼ teaspoon of salt. Repeat with the remaining dough circles.

Using a pizza cutter or a sharp knife, cut each circle into 12 equal wedges (cut the circle into quarters, and each quarter into 3 wedges). Starting at the widest part of one wedge, roll it toward the center to form the rugelach.

Place the rugelach, point side down, onto the prepared sheet pan. Repeat with the remaining wedges, placing them 1½ to 2 inches apart. Refrigerate the rugelach for 30 to 45 minutes.

Preheat the oven to 350°F.

Make the wash Combine the non-dairy milk and maple syrup. Brush each rugelach with the maple syrup mixture. Sprinkle with flaky salt. Bake for 15 to 17 minutes, or until golden. Transfer to a wire rack to cool.

> **NOTE:** I find that soy-based cream cheese works best in baking, like Daiya or Tofutti brands.
>
> **VARIATION:** Add 3 tablespoons of unsweetened shredded coconut to the filling.
>
> **SUBSTITUTION:** If you eat dairy, substitute the vegan alternatives for their dairy counterparts.

WHAT IS RUGELACH? The word *rugelach* loosely translates to "little twists" in Yiddish. Israeli and North American rugelach differ greatly. The Yiddish version is closer in taste and texture to babka, and the North American version is a short, tender cookie rolled around a filling. North American rugelach is made with cream cheese or sour cream in the dough. The addition of cream cheese creates a tender dough that is much easier to handle in comparison with yeasted doughs. Israeli-style rugelach uses a laminated, buttery dough that is leavened with yeast and is often brushed with simple syrup.

Classic Yeasted Sufganiyot

MAKES
About 20 donuts

ON THE TABLE IN...
2 hours 15 minutes, including
1 hour 15 minutes of resting time

Every Hanukkah, my mom would make us homemade sufganiyot—there was never a commercially made donut in sight. We would prep the dough, let it rise, roll, cut, fry, and fill them, and then we'd eat them until we were stuffed to the brim. Piping-hot sufganiyot were always met with fanfare, because her recipe was irresistible and worth fussing over. I took my family recipe and veganized it, resulting in an airy donut stuffed with jam. I love using strawberry jam or grape jelly, but try stuffing these little beauties with vanilla pudding, lemon curd, or date caramel.

Combine the yeast, granulated sugar, and water in the bowl of a stand mixer or in a medium bowl and let stand for 5 minutes. The yeast should dissolve and small bubbles should form on the surface. If not, you may need fresher yeast!

Add the oil and vanilla and whisk until combined.

Attach the dough hook to the stand mixer. Add the flour, orange zest, and salt and mix on low speed until a smooth and elastic dough forms, 7 to 9 minutes. The dough will be tacky but shouldn't stick to the sides of the bowl.

Cover the bowl with a damp, clean kitchen towel or plastic wrap and let rise in a warm place for 45 minutes to 1 hour, until doubled in size. You can also let it rise overnight in the refrigerator.

Line a sheet pan with parchment paper. Lightly flour a work surface. Roll out the rough to ¼ inch thickness. Using a 2½- to 3-inch biscuit cutter or a floured glass, cut the dough into circles and place them on the prepared sheet pan. Let rise for an additional 15 minutes.

In a large, heavy pot, heat the frying oil to 350°F, using a deep-fry or candy thermometer to check the temperature. Set up a cooling rack layered with a paper towel beside the stove.

Spoon the jelly into a squeeze bottle, a piping bag, or a zip-top plastic bag.

continued

- 2¼ teaspoons (7g envelope) instant yeast
- 2 tablespoons granulated sugar
- ¾ cup lukewarm water
- 2 tablespoons neutral oil, such as grapeseed or avocado
- 1 tablespoon vanilla extract
- 2 cups all-purpose flour, plus more as needed
- 1½ teaspoons orange zest
- ½ teaspoon sea salt
- 2 quarts vegetable oil, for frying
- 1 cup seedless jam or jelly or your favorite filling
- ½ cup powdered sugar, for serving

Using a spatula, transfer the dough circles, one at a time, into the hot oil. Flip them gently in the oil. Fry up to 4 at a time, for 75 to 90 seconds per side, or until deeply golden. If the oil is not hot enough, it will take longer to cook and the donuts will be greasy; if the oil is too hot, the donuts will cook much quicker and can burn on the outside, with a raw center. Remove the sufganiyot from the oil using tongs or a spider and transfer them to the wire rack lined with paper towel. I like to use two offset spatulas or chopsticks to flip them in the oil. Let the oil come back to 350°F between batches.

Once slightly cooled, use a straw or chopstick to poke a hole into the center of each sufganiyot. Using the squeeze bottle, squeeze the jam into each one. If using a piping bag or zip-top plastic bag, snip the end or corner off the bag and squeeze into the sufganiyot.

Using a sifter or strainer, dust the sufganiyot with powdered sugar right before serving.

NOTE: Sufganiyot are best served fresh. If you have any leftovers, they will keep for up to 1 day in an airtight container.

VARIATION: Air fry the sufganiyot at 375°F for 7 to 8 minutes, until golden brown.

FEAR OF FRYING

Frying can feel intimidating, but with a few helpful hints, you'll be frying like a pro.

- Use a deep, heavy-bottomed pot.
- Use a candy or digital thermometer to ensure the temperature stays between 350°F and 375°F. To maintain the temperature, don't crowd the pan (sufganiyot should float in a single layer), and let the oil come back to the correct temperature between batches.
- Use a slotted spoon, a spider, tongs, or chopsticks to flip and remove the sufganiyot from the oil.
- Don't multitask! It is easy to over- or under-fry sufganiyot, so be sure to keep a watchful eye on them.

Salted Honey Apple Fritters

MAKES	ON THE TABLE IN...	
12	1 hour	

While I typically associate fried foods (like donuts) with Hanukkah, there's no wrong time to enjoy a hot, fresh-from-the-oil donut. Suited for both Hanukkah and Rosh Hashanah, these fritters come together in an hour or less, using just baking powder as the leavening agent. They are packed with tart apples and drizzled with a salted honey glaze (and are vegan if you use agave syrup instead of honey), for a sticky and sweet New Year treat.

Line a sheet pan with a paper towel. Top with a wire rack. Set aside.

Make the fritters In a large bowl, combine the flour, baking powder, ginger, cinnamon, nutmeg and salt.

In a medium bowl, whisk together the non-dairy milk, brown sugar, ground flax seeds, lemon juice, and vanilla. Let sit for 5 minutes.

Pour the liquid ingredients into the flour mixture and mix with a spatula until just combined. Add the apples and stir until just combined.

In a large, tall-sided skillet, heat 2 inches of oil to 350°F over medium-high heat, using a candy or digital-read thermometer to check the temperature.

Once the oil reaches the correct temperature, add a small piece of batter to the skillet. It should sizzle immediately on contact. If it doesn't, check the temperature again and make sure it has reached 350°F.

Using a scant ¼-cup measure or an ice cream scoop, scoop up the batter and gently drop it into the oil, loosening it from the measuring cup with a spoon if needed.

Fry in small batches of about 4 at a time for 2 to 3 minutes per side, until golden. Using a slotted spoon or tongs, transfer the fritters to the prepared sheet pan.

continued

FRITTERS
1½ cups all-purpose flour

4 teaspoons baking powder

1 teaspoon ground ginger

½ teaspoon ground cinnamon

¼ teaspoon ground nutmeg

¼ teaspoon salt

¾ cup plain unsweetened non-dairy milk

2 tablespoons brown sugar

2 tablespoons ground flax seeds

1 tablespoon lemon juice

1 teaspoon vanilla extract

2 large Granny Smith apples, peeled, cored, and cut into ¼-inch pieces (about 3 cups)

Vegetable oil, for frying

SALTED HONEY GLAZE
2 cups powdered sugar, sifted

2 to 4 tablespoons plain unsweetened non-dairy milk

3 tablespoons honey

½ teaspoon salt

Flaky salt, for serving

Repeat with the remaining batter, rechecking the oil temperature as you go. You may need to adjust the heat to maintain the proper temperature.

Make the glaze In a medium bowl, whisk together the powdered sugar, 2 tablespoons of non-dairy milk, honey, and salt. Add more milk as needed to reach the consistency of heavy cream. Drizzle the glaze over the slightly cooled fritters and sprinkle with flaky salt. Serve immediately.

NOTE: You can prepare the batter up to 1 day in advance and refrigerate in an airtight container. You can store the fried fritters, unglazed, in an airtight container at room temperature for up to 3 days. Glaze them just before serving. However, the fritters are best enjoyed the day they are made.

SUBSTITUTION: Use agave syrup instead of honey for a vegan version.

IS HONEY VEGAN?
Most vegans view honey as non-vegan, but some choose to include honey in their diet. Many vegans believe that harvesting and farming honey is harmful to the bee population. With that said, if you are making these for a crowd, be sure to ask whether your guests include honey in their diet. Some alternatives to honey include maple syrup, molasses, brown rice syrup, date syrup, bee-free "honee," and agave syrup.

WHAT IS BUCKWHEAT HONEY? Buckwheat honey has a unique flavor profile that is earthy, somewhat savory, and has hints of molasses notes. Unlike other honeys, it is dark in color, giving this honey cake a rich, deep-brown hue. It can be challenging to find but worth the search! Try a specialty organic or health food store, or an Eastern European grocer.

Buckwheat Honey Cake

SERVES
8

ON THE TABLE IN...
1 hour 35 minutes

Honey cake is traditionally served during Rosh Hashanah to symbolize hopes and wishes for a sweet New Year. In our household growing up, honey cake was exclusively made with buckwheat honey. It was a dark brown that bordered on black. I reimagined the honey cake of my youth, with buckwheat flour, a splash of whiskey, shredded carrots for moisture, and spicy candied ginger for a cake that can be served during Rosh Hashanah and wintery holidays alike.

Preheat the oven to 350°F. Generously grease a 9-by-5-inch loaf pan and line it with parchment paper.

Make the cake In a mug or heatproof liquid measuring cup, steep the tea in the hot water. Set it aside to cool slightly. Meanwhile, grate the carrots using the largest hole on a box grater. Set aside.

In a large bowl, combine the all-purpose flour, buckwheat flour, baking powder, baking soda, cinnamon, ginger, and salt.

In a separate medium bowl, whisk together the cooled tea, oil, honey, eggs, whiskey, vanilla, orange zest, and grated carrots.

Pour the wet ingredients into the dry, using a rubber spatula to stir until just combined. Fold in the crystallized ginger.

Pour the batter into the prepared loaf pan and bake for 60 to 70 minutes, or until a toothpick comes out clean, turning the loaf pan halfway through the cooking time.

Let cool completely before glazing.

Make the glaze In a bowl, whisk together the powdered sugar, lemon juice, ginger, and salt until smooth. Add 1 to 2 teaspoons of water if needed to thin it out.

Drizzle the glaze over the cake and top with additional crystallized ginger, if desired.

> **NOTES:** Honey cake is always better the next day. Store it at room temperature in an airtight container for up to 4 days. Glaze right before serving. Store leftovers wrapped in plastic wrap and foil in the freezer for up to 3 months.

CAKE

1 black tea bag
⅔ cup hot water
3 medium carrots, peeled
1½ cups all-purpose flour
½ cup buckwheat flour
1 teaspoon baking powder
1 teaspoon baking soda
1 tablespoon ground cinnamon
2 teaspoons ground ginger
½ teaspoon kosher salt
½ cup neutral oil, such as avocado or grapeseed
1 cup buckwheat honey or ¾ cup + 2 tablespoons honey
2 large eggs
2 tablespoons whiskey or apple juice
2 teaspoons vanilla extract
2 teaspoons orange zest
¾ cup chopped crystallized ginger, plus more for garnish

GLAZE (OPTIONAL)

1½ cups powdered sugar
2 tablespoon lemon juice
¾ teaspoon ground ginger
Pinch sea salt

Aunty Ethel's Jammy Apple Cake

SERVES
8

ON THE TABLE IN…
1 hour 30 minutes

My great Aunty Ethel was a spitfire, and we were connected by a shared birthday, despite our generations apart. I would visit her in Vancouver, Canada, where she would share embarrassing stories about my grandpa Louis (her younger brother). She would always make me something vegetarian and dairy-free to eat, including her famous apple cake. Hers was different from any I had ever had; dolloped with golden apricot jam, it was a snacking cake that was studded with apples. I tried to stay true to her recipe by loading it full of apples and a touch of spicy ginger. It's also sweetened with apricot jam in the batter and on the top. This one's for you, Ethel.

5 medium Granny Smith apples, peeled, cored, and cut into ¼-inch pieces (about 6 cups)

2¼ cups all-purpose flour

½ teaspoon ground cinnamon

1 tablespoon baking powder

¼ teaspoon sea salt

2 large eggs

⅔ cup apricot jam, divided

½ cup neutral oil, such as avocado or grapeseed

⅓ cup cold water

⅓ cup sugar

1 tablespoon vanilla extract

2 teaspoons freshly grated ginger

Preheat the oven to 350°F. Grease an 8-inch springform pan and line it with parchment paper.

In a large bowl, combine the apples, flour, cinnamon, baking powder, and salt and mix to combine.

In a separate bowl, whisk together the eggs, ⅓ cup of the apricot jam, oil, cold water, sugar, vanilla, and ginger and add it to the apple and flour mixture, using a rubber spatula to fold in the ingredients until just combined.

Transfer the batter to the cake pan, spreading it with a silicone spatula in an even layer. Dollop the remaining ⅓ cup of apricot jam on top with an offset spatula.

Bake for 55 to 65 minutes, or until a toothpick inserted into the center comes out clean and the cake is deeply golden.

Let cool in the springform pan on a wire rack. Loosen the cake using an offset spatula or butter knife and remove from the pan before serving.

NOTE: Tightly wrap leftovers in plastic wrap and store in the refrigerator for up to 5 days or in the freezer for up to 3 months.

VARIATION: Replace the apricot jam with apple butter.

SUBSTITUTIONS: Replace the fresh ginger with 1½ teaspoons of ground ginger.

APPLES AND HONEY The tradition of dipping apples into honey and saying "Shana Tova U'metukah" symbolizes the wish for "a good and sweet New Year." Honey is often thought to represent the land of Israel. Apple cake is a common menu item during the High Holidays. A classic Jewish Ashkenazi dessert, it is made with oil in lieu of butter or dairy (making it pareve) and is thought to have originated in Poland. Interestingly enough, it is most commonly found in the state of Pennsylvania!

Olive Oil, Pistachio, and Ricotta Cornmeal Sheet Cake

SERVES 16 to 20	ON THE TABLE IN... 2 hours 30 minutes, including at least 1 hour cooling time

Inspired by the Romanian cornmeal-based malai cake, this dairy-packed cake is perfect for celebrating Shavuot or to serve with any springtime menu. Malai cake is sweet, often made using a curd cheese, with a crumbly texture that is a mix between a cake and cornbread.

Preheat the oven to 325°F. Lightly coat a 9-by-13-inch baking dish with nonstick spray and line it with parchment paper, leaving an overhang on the long sides.

Make the cake In a medium bowl, whisk together the flour, cornmeal, pistachios, baking powder, baking soda, and salt.

In a separate bowl, combine the granulated sugar, vanilla, olive oil, Greek yogurt, ricotta, and eggs. Add the wet ingredients to the dry ingredients and use a rubber spatula to fold them together until just combined. Scrape the batter into the prepared baking dish and smooth the surface.

Bake for 35 to 40 minutes, rotating the pan halfway through, until the cake is golden and a tester inserted into the center comes out clean. Let the cake cool in the pan on a wire rack for at least 1 hour.

Make the whipped cream Using a hand mixer or a stand mixer fitted with the whisk attachment, whip the whipping cream, powdered sugar, vanilla, and lemon zest on medium speed until medium peaks form. If you overwhip, add a splash of additional whipping cream to the bowl and gently fold to combine. Cover and let sit in the fridge until ready to use.

Carefully run an offset spatula or paring knife around the sides of the cake and use the parchment paper as a handle to lift the cake from the pan; remove the parchment. Cut the cake into squares and serve topped with whipped cream, chopped pistachios, a drizzle of olive oil, and dollop with lemon curd, using a knife to swirl into the whipped cream.

CAKE

- 1½ cups all-purpose flour
- 1½ cups yellow cornmeal
- 1 cup shelled unsalted pistachios, finely chopped
- 1 tablespoon baking powder
- ½ teaspoon baking soda
- ½ teaspoon kosher salt
- 1¼ cups granulated sugar
- 1 tablespoon vanilla extract
- 1 cup extra-virgin olive oil
- 1 cup plain full-fat Greek yogurt
- 1 cup whole-milk ricotta
- 4 large eggs

WHIPPED CREAM

- 1 cup heavy whipping cream, plus more as needed
- 2 tablespoons powdered sugar
- ½ teaspoon vanilla extract
- ¼ teaspoon lemon zest

TO SERVE

- ¼ cup shelled pistachios, finely chopped
- 1 tablespoon extra-virgin olive oil
- Lemon curd, store-bought

NOTE: The cake can be stored tightly wrapped at room temperature for 2 days or frozen for up to 2 weeks.

Halvah Pistachio Babka Rolls

MAKES	ON THE TABLE IN...	
12	4 hours, including at least 3 hours resting time	

Babka is a yeasted, enriched sweet bread that is rolled and twisted with sweet fillings like chocolate, nuts, or spices, baked, and then drenched in a sweet syrup. Traditionally, babka is baked in a loaf pan and cut into slices to reveal a stunning pattern of sweet filling. Inspired by my travels to Sweden and sampling their cardamom buns, I wanted to make a personal-size babka. The key to great babka is the twists and coiling, and making these knotted rolls with their sweet pistachio filling is a fun play on the classic babka loaf.

DOUGH

2 cups bread flour, plus more as needed

½ cup whole wheat flour

2 tablespoons sugar

2¼ teaspoons (7g envelope) instant yeast

½ teaspoon kosher salt

1 cup lukewarm plain unsweetened non-dairy milk

1 tablespoon vanilla extract

⅓ cup vegan butter, at room temperature, cubed

FILLING

1¼ cups shelled unsalted pistachios

1 cup crumbled halvah, divided

⅓ cup vegan butter, at room temperature

¼ cup sugar

1 tablespoon neutral oil

1 teaspoon ground cardamom

1 teaspoon vanilla extract

½ teaspoon sea salt

¼ teaspoon almond extract

SYRUP

¼ cup sugar

¼ cup water

Make the dough Combine the bread flour, whole wheat flour, sugar, yeast, and salt in the bowl of a stand mixer fitted with the dough hook. Mix until combined. Add the non-dairy milk and vanilla and mix on medium-low speed until a dough forms, 4 to 5 minutes. The dough will be somewhat smooth and sticky.

With the mixer running, add the cubed vegan butter slowly, until all the butter is incorporated and a smooth, shiny dough forms, scraping down the sides of the bowl as needed, about 10 minutes. The dough will be elastic and tacky.

Oil a large bowl and set it aside.

Lightly oil your hands and transfer the dough to the oiled bowl. Cover with plastic wrap and let rise in a warm spot until doubled in size, about 1 hour. You can let this rise in the refrigerator overnight, which will give it a richer flavor.

Make the filling In a food processor or high-powered blender, combine the pistachios, ⅓ cup of the halvah, vegan butter, sugar, oil, cardamom, vanilla, salt, and almond extract and blend until smooth.

Generously grease a 12-cup muffin tin with neutral oil. Line with cupcake liners, if desired. Line a large sheet pan with parchment or wax paper.

continued

Form the rolls Once risen, punch down the dough to remove any air bubbles.

On a floured surface or wax paper, use a rolling pin to roll out the dough into a 12-by-24-inch rectangle. Spread the filling in an even layer using a spatula. Sprinkle with the remaining ⅔ cup of halvah.

Fold the dough like an envelope: Fold the bottom third of the dough closest to you up, and then fold the top third over it. Use the rolling pin to roll it into a 10-by-12-inch rectangle.

Transfer the dough to the prepared sheet pan and refrigerate for 20 minutes. Cooled dough is easier to handle.

Using a pizza wheel or a knife, cut the chilled dough into 1-by-10-inch strips. Gently tap the dough strip on the kitchen counter and pull each end gently to elongate the dough. Twist the strip to show the layers and wrap it around your index and middle finger to create a spiral. Tuck the end into the center of the spiral. Place in one of the muffin cups, twisted side up. Repeat with the remaining strips of dough.

Cover the muffin tin with a clean kitchen towel and let the dough rise for an additional 20 to 30 minutes while the oven preheats.

Preheat the oven to 350°F.

Bake the babka for 18 to 22 minutes, or until deeply golden and a thermometer inserted into the center reads 190°F.

Make the syrup Combine the sugar and water in a small saucepan over medium-high heat, stirring to fully dissolve the sugar, until just boiling.

After removing the babka from the oven, use a pastry brush to immediately brush them with the syrup; it may feel like too much, but be sure to use it all!

> **NOTE:** Babka can't be rushed; it needs time to rise, rest, and bake, so be sure to budget enough time to make it. Prepare the dough up to 1 day in advance (up until the first rise) and the filling up to 3 days in advance. Babka is best enjoyed the day it's made, though it can be stored in an airtight container at room temperature for up to 3 days.

BAKING BABKA

With roots in Jewish communities in Poland and Ukraine, babka is widely popular in Israel. Babka gets its name from the term for "grandmother," *bubbe* or *babcia*. The treat came from humble origins, where extra challah dough was rolled around sweet fillings and baked as a dessert or to give to children while they waited for Shabbat. Babka is a popular dish to eat for break-fast or for a decadent breakfast or afternoon tea. No matter when you eat it or where you bring it, I always think of *Seinfeld*, when Jerry says, "You can't beat a babka!"

Vegan Tahini Olive Oil Challah

MAKES	ON THE TABLE IN...
One 1-pound loaf	3 hours, including 1 hour 30 minutes resting time

Challah is full of symbolism. It is enjoyed when signifying the start of Shabbat. A six-strand challah (or two three-stranded challahs) is thought to symbolize the six workdays of the week, with the three strands representing truth, peace, and justice, while a round challah signifies continuity during the New Year. No matter how you interpret it, there's no denying that challah is something to look forward to each week. It is traditionally made with eggs and/or butter, but I created this vegan alternative to the classic Shabbat loaf. This recipe uses tahini to replace the richness of eggs, is sweetened with maple syrup, and gets a slightly golden color from the olive oil. It is my go-to Friday-night challah.

Oil a medium bowl and set aside.

Combine the yeast, sugar, and water in the bowl of a stand mixer. Let sit until the yeast starts to foam or "bloom," 5 to 10 minutes. If the yeast does not bloom, you may need to get fresher yeast. Add the olive oil and tahini and mix to combine. Attach the dough hook to the stand mixer.

Add the flour, 1 cup at a time, while mixing on low speed. Add the salt with the last ½ cup of flour and mix until a dough forms. Increase the speed to medium and knead the dough until smooth, 6 to 7 minutes. It will be somewhat sticky. Alternatively, you can knead by hand for 8 to 10 minutes. It should be a smooth dough to ensure the strands are smooth for easy shaping.

Transfer the dough to the oiled bowl. Cover with a clean, damp kitchen towel and let the dough rise in a warm place until doubled in size, about 1 hour.

Preheat the oven to 350°F. Line a sheet pan with parchment paper.

Punch down the dough. Divide the dough into 3 or 4 equal pieces, depending on the braid style you plan to use. Rolling the dough should not require any flour. Roll the dough into ropes that are tapered on both ends for best results.

continued

2¼ teaspoons (7g envelope) instant yeast

¼ cup sugar

1¼ cups lukewarm water

3 tablespoons extra-virgin olive oil, plus more as needed

2 tablespoons tahini

3½ cups bread flour

1 teaspoon sea salt

1 tablespoon maple syrup

1 tablespoon plain unsweetened non-dairy milk

3 tablespoons sesame or poppy seeds (optional)

Braid according to your preference. Transfer the braided loaf to the prepared sheet pan, cover with a clean, damp kitchen towel, and let the dough rise until slightly puffy, 20 to 30 minutes. To test whether it is proofed, press your finger into the dough—it should not bounce back fully.

In a small bowl, whisk together the maple syrup and non-dairy milk. Brush the dough gently with the mixture and top with seeds, if using.

Bake for 40 to 45 minutes, turning the sheet pan halfway through. Let cool on the sheet pan.

NOTE: Challah can be prepared up to 24 hours in advance. Follow the directions through the braiding step and place the braided loaf on a parchment-lined sheet pan. Tent with plastic wrap and let it rise overnight in the refrigerator. Let it come to room temperature for 45 to 60 minutes before baking. For braiding tips, see the instructions for Classic One-Bowl Challah (page 208).

VARIATION: Make these into challah buns by braiding 8 smaller loaves and baking them until golden, 15 to 20 minutes.

ALL ABOUT CHALLAH Every time I teach a challah-baking class, participants lament that they have always been too intimidated to try it on their own. Challah doesn't have to be complicated. Here are my top tips for making challah:

- Using all-purpose flour in place of bread flour will yield a wetter dough due to its lower protein content. You may need to add extra flour.
- Don't overdo the flour; your dough should be tacky, but not sticky. Adding too much flour will result in a dense loaf. Remember, you can always add more flour, but you can't take it away! If the dough feels too crumbly, add 1 to 2 teaspoons of oil.
- Give it time. Yeasted dough needs time to proof (rise); rushing it will yield a dense, brick-like loaf.
- Let the dough rest in a warm spot, covered, or overnight in the refrigerator.
- The dough has proofed enough when you can quickly press your pointer finger into the dough and it does not refill to its original shape, instead holding the indentation. If the dough bounces back quickly, it needs more time.

Classic One-Bowl Challah

MAKES
One 1-pound challah

ON THE TABLE IN...
3 hours, including 1 hour 30 minutes
resting time

No Friday-night dinner is complete without challah. My ideal challah is sweet, a little doughy, a deep golden brown, and topped with toasted seeds. My grandma Eva would make challah into individual shaped buns, one for each of us! It was her special way to welcome Shabbat and it's one of my favorite ways to make challah. It also makes the best sandwiches! This recipe is great for weeknight baking, taking only a few hours to make the subtly sweet dough using just one bowl.

DOUGH

3¼ to 3½ cups bread flour, plus
    more as needed

2¼ teaspoons (7g envelope)
    instant yeast

1 teaspoon kosher salt

⅔ cup lukewarm water

2 large eggs, at room temperature

1 egg yolk

3 tablespoons olive oil, plus more
    as needed

3 tablespoons honey or agave
    syrup

EGG WASH

1 large egg, whisked

1 tablespoon water

Toppings (see Variations,
    page 211)

Make the dough Oil a large bowl and set aside.

In a large bowl, combine 3¼ cups of the bread flour, yeast, and salt and stir until well mixed. Add the water, eggs, egg yolk, olive oil, and honey and use a wooden spoon to mix until a rough dough forms. Turn the dough out onto a floured work surface and knead until a soft dough forms, 8 to 10 minutes. The dough should be tacky and a little sticky. If the dough is too sticky, add up to ¼ cup of bread flour. If the dough is too dry, add 1 to 2 tablespoons of water. A dry challah dough means a dense challah! You can also do this in your stand mixer using the dough hook and mix on low speed for 6 to 8 minutes.

Once the dough is smooth, transfer it to the oiled bowl and cover with a clean, damp kitchen towel. Let rise in a warm place until doubled in size, about 1 hour. Or let it rise in the refrigerator overnight.

Preheat the oven to 350°F. Line a sheet pan with parchment paper.

To check whether the dough has properly proofed, poke it with your index finger. If the dough just rebounds, it is ready. If it rebounds immediately, check again in 10 to 15 minutes.

Punch down dough to remove any air bubbles and transfer to a floured surface. Cut the dough into 3 or 4 equal pieces, depending on the braid style you plan to use. Roll each piece into a rope that is 12 to 14 inches long and tapered on both ends.

continued

Braid the ropes together, pinching them together at the ends and tucking them under.

Cover with a clean, damp kitchen towel and let the dough rise until slightly puffy, 20 to 25 minutes. To test whether it is proofed, press your finger into the dough; it should not bounce back fully.

Make the egg wash In a small bowl, whisk together the egg and water. Brush the dough with the egg wash and sprinkle your favorite topping over the top.

Bake for 40 minutes, turning the sheet pan halfway through. Let cool on the sheet pan for 30 minutes.

NOTE: To store challah, seal it in an airtight zip-top plastic bag or a bread bag for up to 5 days.

VARIATIONS: Top your challah with different seeds and toppings:
- Everything Bagel: Top with 3 tablespoons of Everything Bagel Spice (page 246).
- Pizza Challah: Brush with 3 tablespoons of tomato sauce instead of the egg wash. Top with ¼ cup of shredded mozzarella cheese.
- Cinnamon Toast: Mix 2 tablespoons of sugar and 1 teaspoon of cinnamon and sprinkle over the top.
- Coconut Almond: Mix 1 tablespoon of shredded unsweetened coconut, 2 tablespoons of sliced almonds, and 1 teaspoon of sugar. Sprinkle the mixture over the top.
- Unicorn Challah: Top with ¼ cup of rainbow sprinkles.

SHAPING CHALLAH

Challah can come in many shapes and sizes, from round, to 3 strands, to 9 strands, and beyond. In fact, among many Jewish people, challah doesn't need to be braided at all! Here are some of my tips for shaping challah:
- Ensure your dough is smooth, as this is often the issue when rolling!
- Use a kitchen scale to ensure the strands are the same size.
- Avoid using flour when rolling the dough.
- When rolling the strands, make them slightly wider in the center and tapered at the outer edges.
- Tuck the ends underneath the loaf to seal in the braid.

Israeli Everything Pita Bread

MAKES	ON THE TABLE IN…
10	2 hours, including 1 hour 10 minutes resting time

In Israel, nearly every meal includes a creamy bowl of hummus served with fluffy pita bread. Pita, famous for its pockets, is a staple in Middle Eastern cuisine, served with meals for sopping up sauces, scooping up hummus, or enveloping crispy falafel or tender, fried eggplant. This recipe is based on my cousin Yossi's recipe for Israeli-style pita, our family favorite. This version is coated with everything bagel spice on one side and baked until puffed.

2¼ teaspoons (7g envelope) instant yeast

1½ cups lukewarm water

1 teaspoon sugar

3 to 3¼ cups all-purpose flour, plus more as needed

2 teaspoons olive oil

½ teaspoon salt

1 cup Everything Bagel Spice (page 246) or store-bought

Oil a large bowl and set aside.

Combine the yeast, water, and sugar in the bowl of a stand mixer or medium bowl and stir until mixed. Let stand for 5 minutes. The yeast should dissolve and small bubbles should form on the surface. If not, you may need fresher yeast!

Add 3 cups of flour, olive oil, and salt and mix on low speed until a smooth dough forms, 6 to 8 minutes. Add the remaining ¼ cup of flour if the dough is too wet. If making the dough by hand, once a shaggy dough forms, turn out the dough onto a lightly floured surface and knead until a smooth dough forms, 10 to 12 minutes.

Once the dough is smooth, transfer it to the oiled bowl and cover with a clean, damp kitchen towel or plastic wrap. Let rise in a warm place until the dough doubles in size, about 1 hour.

Punch down the dough to remove any air bubbles. Using a knife or bench scraper, divide the dough into 10 equal pieces and shape them each into balls. Cover with a kitchen towel and let rest for 10 minutes.

Preheat the oven to 475°F. If you have a pizza stone, place it in the oven to heat. Alternatively, you can place a cast-iron pan or a heavy sheet pan in the oven. Cut ten 8-by-8-inch squares of parchment paper.

continued

On a floured work surface and using a floured rolling pin, roll one of the balls of dough into an 8-inch circle about ¼ inch thick. Repeat with the remaining pieces of dough.

Fill a shallow, round dish or cake pan with ½ inch of water. Pour the everything bagel spice onto a large flat plate.

Dip one side of a dough circle into the water briefly and place it, water side down, into the bagel spice mixture to coat.

Place the dough, spice side down, onto one of the pieces of parchment paper and repeat with the remaining dough circles.

Slide each circle of dough along with the parchment paper, spice side down, onto the pizza stone or cast-iron pan in the oven and close the oven door immediately. Bake for 2 to 3 minutes, or until puffy and just beginning to brown. Flip over the pita and cook for 1 minute more. As the pitas cook, your parchment paper may burn; replace as needed. You may be able to bake only 1 or 2 pitas at one a time.

Place the pita on a clean kitchen towel. Repeat with the remaining dough circles.

NOTE: A pizza stone is best for cooking this pita. If your pita does not puff up, the pizza stone or cast-iron pan may not be hot enough. Be sure to cook the pita with the seeded side down, which will help it puff up and create a pocket. Store the baked pita in a zip-top plastic bag for up to 3 days at room temperature.

VARIATION: Use sesame seeds instead of bagel spice, or omit the seeds entirely.

ISRAELI-STYLE PITA BREAD

Typically thicker than other flatbreads or pitas, Israeli pita is soft and doughy, and when made correctly, it contains a pocket, which is perfect for stuffing with ingredients like my Baked Herby Falafel Balls (page 151).

Mini Montreal Bagels

MAKES
20

ON THE TABLE IN...
2 hours, including 40 minutes of
resting time

*Bagels are a hot topic in the world of Jewish cuisine. People proclaim themselves either team
Montreal or team New York style (not to mention the Jerusalem bagel and newer Bay Area bagel),
and it is an argument you are guaranteed to lose, no matter which side you are on. Let me preface
this by saying that as a Canadian American, I am a die-hard Montreal bagel lover. No other bagel
will do. So, on that note, these are Montreal-inspired bagels, with a sweet, dense dough rather than
the more fluffy New York–style bagels. Mini bagels are my favorite way to brunch, piled high with
(vegan) cream cheese, avocado, or peanut butter.*

Make the dough In the bowl of a stand mixer or a large bowl,
combine the water, sugar, and yeast and mix well. Let sit until the
yeast starts to foam or "bloom," 5 to 10 minutes. If the yeast does
not bloom, you may need to get fresher yeast.

Add the maple syrup, olive oil, bread flour, and salt.

Attach the dough hook to the stand mixer and mix on low speed
until smooth and elastic, 4 to 5 minutes. Note: This dough will be
dry and stiff; if the stand mixer cannot handle the dough, knead
by hand on a floured surface until smooth, 8 to 10 minutes.

Lightly grease a large bowl with oil. Place the dough in the bowl,
turning to coat. Cover the bowl with plastic wrap and a clean
kitchen towel and let rise in a warm spot until it rises slightly,
about 30 minutes. You are not looking for it to be doubled in
size. The shortened rise time allows for a denser, Montreal-style
bagel. For a fluffier bagel, let the dough rise for 60 minutes.

Line 2 large sheet pans with parchment paper.

When the dough has risen, punch it down to remove any air
bubbles. Divide the dough into 20 equal pieces, each about
1½ ounces, or slightly larger than a golf ball.

continued

DOUGH

1 cup lukewarm water

1 tablespoon sugar

2¼ teaspoons (7g envelope)
   instant yeast

3 tablespoons maple syrup

3 tablespoons extra-virgin
   olive oil

3 cups bread flour

1½ teaspoons sea salt

TOPPING

1 cup sesame seeds, poppy
   seeds, or Everything Bagel
   Spice (page 246) or store-
   bought (optional)

WATER BATH

8 to 10 cups water

¼ cup agave syrup, maple syrup,
   or honey

THE SUBTLETIES OF THE BAGEL

Compared to New York bagels, Montreal bagels are denser, chewier, and sweeter. They are also smaller than New York bagels, boiled in honey water, and wood-fired for a golden crust. New York bagels are boiled in water (often with barley malt) and baked on burlap-covered boards. New Yorkers will say that the water makes the bagel, and the distinctive water in New York is the secret ingredient to making the best bagels.

Roll the dough into balls and let them sit for 5 minutes to allow the gluten to relax. Using your index finger, poke a hole in the center of each dough ball, twirling it with your finger on the counter to expand the hole and create a mini bagel shape about 3 inches in diameter. You can also shape the bagels by forming a 9-inch rope and attaching the ends, but I find that for mini bagels, this method is simpler. Note that Montreal bagels have a larger hole than New York–style bagels.

Transfer the mini bagels to the prepared sheet pan, cover with a clean kitchen towel, and let rest for 10 minutes.

Preheat the oven to 425°F.

Make the topping Pour your choice of seed topping into a shallow bowl.

Prepare the water bath In a large, wide, tall-sided saucepan, combine the water and agave. There should be 4 to 5 inches of water in the pan. Bring it to a boil over high heat.

Lower the heat to medium-high. Carefully place 3 or 4 mini bagels into the water bath and boil for 30 seconds. Using two spatulas, a frying spider, or a set of silicone-tipped tongs, flip over the bagels and boil for another 30 seconds. Remove the bagels from the water bath, making sure to shake off any excess water. If the bagels are very wet, lightly pat them dry with a paper towel. You need some moisture for the seeds to stick.

Transfer the boiled bagel to the seeds and coat it on both sides. Transfer the bagel to the prepared sheet pan. Repeat with the rest of the bagels.

Bake for 15 to 17 minutes, turning the sheet pan halfway through, until deeply golden. If using two racks, alternate the sheet pans so the bagels will brown evenly.

Let cool for 10 minutes on the sheet pan.

NOTE: Homemade bagels are best eaten the day they are made, but if there are extras, store them in a zip-top plastic bag, squeezing out any excess air before sealing the bag. Store at room temperature for up to 3 days. Bagels can also be frozen in zip-top bags for up to 3 months. I like to preslice the bagels before freezing for easy schmear-ing when ready to eat!

VARIATION: You can make larger bagels by dividing the dough into 10 pieces and shaping them in the same way. Boil for 45 seconds per side, and bake for 22 to 25 minutes.

Sesame Seed Malawach

ON THE TABLE IN...
2 hours 15 minutes,
including 1 hour 30 minutes resting time

Malawach is one of my favorite dishes to eat in Israel. It is a bread, usually served with hard-boiled eggs, grated tomato, Zhoug (page 239), and honey, or it can be made into a wrap and loaded with Baked Herby Falafel Balls (page 151) or Jackfruit and White Bean "Shawarma" (page 125). The magic of malawach is the pull-apart layers that are created by folding and knotting the dough with oil or softened butter. This recipe updates the classic with the addition of sesame seeds, and for an extra richness, I've added butter to the frying pan.

4 cups all-purpose flour

3 tablespoons sesame seeds

1 teaspoon baking powder

1 teaspoon salt

1¼ to 1¾ cups water, divided

½ cup butter or ghee, melted and cooled slightly, plus more for cooking

In a large bowl, combine the flour, sesame seeds, baking powder, and salt. Add 1 cup of the water and mix into a dough. Add the remaining water, ¼ cup at a time, until the mixture comes together into a soft, pliable dough. Using your hands, knead the dough in the bowl until it is soft and smooth, 5 to 6 minutes. It should not be sticky, but it will be slightly tacky to the touch. Cover with a damp kitchen towel and let sit for 30 minutes.

Divide the dough into 10 equal pieces. Cover and let rest for 15 minutes.

Using your fingers, take a piece of dough and press and push the dough away from the center toward the edges and stretch until it is a large rectangle; it's okay if it tears slightly! It should be thin enough to see through the dough. Using a pastry brush, brush the melted butter over the top of the dough.

Starting on the longer side, fold the dough over in 1-inch increments until you have a long rope. Tie the rope into a knot, and knot again, and then tuck the ends underneath the dough.

Transfer the knotted dough to a sheet pan and cover with a kitchen towel for 45 minutes. You can also cover with plastic wrap and store in the refrigerator for up to 5 days.

When ready to cook, use a rolling pin to flatten one of the knotted dough pieces into an 8-inch circle. Repeat with the remaining dough.

Preheat the oven to 200°F.

Heat a cast-iron pan over medium-high heat. When the pan is hot, melt 1 tablespoon of butter. Add one piece of dough and cook until golden brown, 1 to 2 minutes per side, using tongs to flip them over. Repeat with the remaining dough, adding butter each time you cook another piece. Keep the malawach warm in the oven until ready to serve.

NOTE: To make them in advance, prepare the dough until ready to cook. Layer the uncooked malawach between sheets of wax paper, cover in plastic wrap, and freeze or refrigerate. Cook directly from the refrigerator or freezer.

VARIATION: Instead of sesame seeds, use nigella seeds, which have a pleasingly bitter, slightly oniony aroma.

SUBSTITUTION: Use vegan butter or coconut oil, if preferred.

WHAT IS MALAWACH?

Malawach is a traditional flatbread from Yemen that was brought to Israel by Yemenite Jews. Malawach is likely an early version of puff pastry, and it's usually a round, layered dough that is cooked in a hot skillet, resulting in a buttery, flaky flatbread. If it is rolled into cylinders, it becomes *jachnun*.

Homemade Matzo

In my house, matzo is eaten year-round. With the right toppings (such as cream cheese and Everything Bagel Spice, page 246), matzo is one of my go-to snacks. While boxed matzo often leaves a lot to be desired, homemade matzo is in a league of its own, with an irresistibly toasted flavor and endless variations. The trick to making matzo is that it must be mixed, rolled, and baked within 18 minutes from the moment the water touches the flour. This is to prevent any leavening or fermenting from occurring. While this matzo wouldn't be strictly kosher for Passover, it does conform to the 18-minute rule.

1 cup all-purpose flour
¼ teaspoon kosher salt
Spices (optional; see Variations)
1 teaspoons extra-virgin olive oil
⅓ cup ½ cup warm water

VARIATIONS:

- Turmeric: ½ teaspoon ground turmeric, ¼ teaspoon ground ginger, ¼ teaspoon black pepper
- Garlic and Herb: 1 teaspoon garlic powder, 1 teaspoon Italian herb blend
- Cinnamon: 1 tablespoon unsalted butter, melted, 1 teaspoon sugar, 1 teaspoon ground cinnamon. Brush the dough with melted butter and top with sugar and cinnamon.

Preheat the oven to 475°F. Set aside a sheet pan. Get out a rolling pin and fork.

In a medium bowl, combine the flour, salt, and any spices, if using. Set your timer to 18 minutes.

Add the oil and ⅓ cup of water to the flour mixture and mix until a dough forms. If the mixture is dry, add more water, 1 tablespoon at a time.

Knead on a clean counter until smooth, 4 to 5 minutes. Divide the dough into 4 equal pieces, each about the size of an egg.

Roll each piece as thin as possible. The thinner, the better. Transfer to the sheet pan. The dough will not expand, so feel free to place them right next to one another. Use a fork to poke holes all over the dough.

Bake for 3 to 4 minutes, or until golden and crisp. Using tongs, carefully flip the matzo over and bake for 1 more minute. It will crisp up as it cools.

NOTE: Store matzo in airtight zip-top plastic bags at room temperature for up to 5 days.

WHAT IS MATZO?

Matzo is an unleavened bread that is eaten during Passover. Made with flour and water, it is baked before it can rise (within 18 minutes). It commemorates the Jews fleeing from Egypt and is a reminder of the rushed exodus, where the Jewish people did not have time to let their bread rise. When buying matzo for Passover, make sure it reads "Kosher for Passover" if you are following Passover traditions. Matzo made with alternative flours, such as spelt, are not suitable.

APPLE AND
HONEY
WHISKEY
SOUR

VEGAN
EGG CREAM

DATE SYRUP
AND HAWAIJ
ESPRESSO
MARTINI

POMEGRANATE
RED WINE
SPRITZER

NEW YORK
SOUR WITH
RED WINE AND
POMEGRANATE
MOLASSES

Cocktails & Beverages

HORSERADISH
BLOODY MARY

HALVAH
MILKSHAKE

OLIVE AND
SUMAC
MARTINI

MULLED
MANISCHEWITZ

Pomegranate Red Wine Spritzer

SERVES	ON THE TABLE IN...	
8	10 minutes	

Shabbat isn't complete without a blessing over a glass of wine. Instead of your typical glass of red, try a lower ABV spritzer, made with pomegranate juice, Aperol, and red wine.

1 (750ml) bottle medium-bodied red wine, like a Merlot or Cabernet Franc

4 ounces Aperol

6 ounces pomegranate juice

1 orange, sliced

4 cups soda water

In a pitcher or glass, stir together the wine, Aperol, and pomegranate juice. Add the sliced orange and top with soda water before serving.

VARIATION: Omit the alcohol and replace with an additional 3 ounces of pomegranate juice per serving and a squeeze of lime juice for a satisfying mocktail.

SPRITZER FOR ONE

SERVES: 1

3 ounces medium-bodied red wine

½ ounce Aperol

1½ ounces pomegranate juice

Orange slice

½ cup soda water

In a glass, stir together the wine, Aperol, and pomegranate juice. Add the orange slice and top with soda water.

Apple and Honey Whiskey Sour

SERVES
1

ON THE TABLE IN...
10 minutes

A cocktail made for Rosh Hashanah, this whiskey sour gets its sweetness from honey and apple juice instead of simple syrup. The egg white creates a beautiful foamy cocktail!

In a cocktail shaker or jar with a lid, combine the whiskey, lemon juice, apple juice, honey, and egg white. Fill with ice.

Seal the lid and shake until well chilled, 20 to 30 seconds. Strain into a cocktail glass and top with a few drops of bitters and an apple slice.

2 ounces whiskey
1 ounce fresh lemon juice
1 ounce apple juice
1 teaspoon honey or agave syrup
1 egg white
Ice
Angostura bitters, to garnish
Apple slice, to garnish

> **VARIATION:** Use 2 tablespoons of aquafaba (see page 22) in place of the egg white for a tasty vegan cocktail.

Olive and Sumac Martini

SERVES
1

ON THE TABLE IN...
10 minutes

Martinis are my beverage of choice, extra dirty and with extra olives. This recipe is my ideal martini, with a pinch of sumac for a hint of zesty, vibrant flavor and color. Add or omit the olive brine to your liking, but if you're like me... double it!

Pour a little olive juice into a shallow dish. Place some sumac in another shallow dish. Dip the rim of a cocktail glass into the olive juice and then into the sumac. Gently shake off any excess sumac and set aside.

In a cocktail shaker or a jar with a lid, combine the gin, vermouth, ½ ounce olive juice, and ½ teaspoon sumac and fill with ice. Stir or seal and shake until well chilled, 20 to 30 seconds. Strain the liquid into the rimmed cocktail glass and garnish with olives.

½ ounce olive juice, plus more to rim the glass
½ teaspoon sumac, plus more to rim the glass
2½ ounces gin or vodka
½ ounce dry vermouth
Ice
2 or 3 olives, pitted

Horseradish Bloody Mary

SERVES
1

ON THE TABLE IN...
10 minutes

The quintessential brunch cocktail, this Bloody Mary gets its kick from horseradish, a dash of liquid smoke, and a za'atar rim. Stuff it to the brim with pickled green beans, asparagus, and everything in between.

Za'atar, to rim the glass

1 lemon wedge

2 ounces vodka

4 ounces tomato juice

½ ounce lemon juice

1 to 2 teaspoons prepared
   horseradish

Pinch black pepper

Dash liquid smoke

TO GARNISH

Celery stalk

Pickled bean or asparagus

Place some za'atar in a shallow dish. Run the edge of a lemon wedge over the rim of a cocktail glass. Dip the rim of the glass in the za'atar and gently shake off any excess. Set the glass aside.

Pour the vodka, tomato juice, lemon juice, horseradish (to taste), pepper, and liquid smoke into the glass. Stir using a cocktail stirrer.

Garnish with a celery stalk and pickled green bean.

VARIATION: Omit the vodka for a refreshing mocktail or try it with gin or even mezcal (in which case, omit the liquid smoke, as mezcal is already smoky) for a different twist.

Mulled Manischewitz

SERVES
5

ON THE TABLE IN...
30 minutes

A warming drink for wintry Shabbats, sweet Manischewitz doesn't need any additional sweetener, just rich aromatic spices and a kick of orange liqueur.

In a medium saucepan, combine the wine, orange liqueur, orange slices, cloves, cardamom, allspice, cinnamon sticks, star anise, and ginger and cook over medium-high heat until it just begins to bubble and simmer.

Decrease the heat to low and simmer for 30 minutes or up to 2 hours. Strain into glasses and serve warm, garnished with a cinnamon stick.

1 (750ml) bottle Manischewitz or sweet kosher wine

2 ounces orange liqueur

1 orange, cut into ¼-inch slices

5 whole cloves

2 cardamom pods

4 allspice berries

2 cinnamon sticks, plus more to garnish

1 star anise

1 slice fresh ginger

New York Sour with Red Wine and Pomegranate Molasses

SERVES
1

ON THE TABLE IN...
10 minutes

This is a twist on the whiskey sour. It's made with a layer of red wine that floats on the surface of the cocktail. A lover of all things sweet and sour, I added tangy pomegranate molasses and sweet kosher wine to boost the flavor profile of this classic. If you can't find sweet kosher wine, try using port.

In a cocktail shaker or jar with a lid, combine the whiskey, lemon juice, maple syrup, and pomegranate molasses and fill with ice. Seal and shake until chilled, 20 to 30 seconds. Strain into a glass over ice.

Slowly pour the wine into the glass over the back of a barspoon, which will cause the wine to float over the top of the drink. Garnish with a lemon twist.

2 ounces whiskey

1 ounce lemon juice

½ ounce maple syrup

½ ounce pomegranate molasses

Ice

½ ounce sweet kosher red wine or port

Lemon twist, to garnish

Vegan Egg Cream

SERVES
1

ON THE TABLE IN...
10 minutes

Egg creams are a Jewish deli classic—a combination of Fox's U-Bet chocolate syrup, milk, and carbonated water (and yes, no actual egg or cream) that tastes like a creamy soda and reminds me of ice cream floats growing up. Every year on the yahrzeit (the anniversary of passing) of my father-in-law, we toast to his legacy with a tall egg cream. Instead of the bottled chocolate sauce, I created a refined sugar–free and vegan version using maple syrup and topped it with non-dairy creamer and soda water for a modern spin on the deli staple.

1 ounce maple syrup

2 teaspoons cocoa powder

¼ teaspoon vanilla extract

Pinch sea salt

2 ounces unsweetened non-dairy creamer

6 to 8 ounces seltzer

In a tall glass, combine the maple syrup, cocoa powder, vanilla, and salt and stir until combined.

Top with the non-dairy creamer. Add the seltzer, stir vigorously, and serve.

COCKTAILS & BEVERAGES

Halvah Milkshake

SERVES
1

ON THE TABLE IN...
10 minutes

I love how customizable milkshakes are. For a classic version, all you need is just milk and ice cream, but my halvah milkshake is anything but that. Creamy vanilla ice cream is blended with tahini, pistachios, and halvah until smooth. The richness of tahini and pistachios cuts through the sweetness of the ice cream for a balanced (but deliciously decadent) treat. To make it vegan, use your favorite vegan vanilla ice cream and milk alternative.

2 scoops vanilla ice cream

4 ounces milk

¼ cup ice

2 tablespoons tahini

2 tablespoons shelled pistachios

3 tablespoons halvah

Whipped cream, for serving

In a blender, combine the vanilla ice cream, milk, ice, tahini, pistachios, and halvah and blend until smooth. Top with whipped cream.

Date Syrup and Hawaij Espresso Martini

SERVES	ON THE TABLE IN...	
1	10 minutes	

Here's a twist on the classic espresso martini with the addition of rich date syrup and warm spiced hawaij. Hawaij is an earthy, spicy Yemenite blend of turmeric, cardamom, coriander, black pepper, and cloves that complements the espresso.

In a shaker or a jar with a lid, combine the vodka, espresso, Kahlúa, hawaij, and date syrup and fill with ice. Seal and shake until very well chilled, 20 to 30 seconds. Strain into a cocktail glass and garnish with the espresso beans.

2 ounces vodka

1½ ounces espresso, cooled

½ ounce Kahlúa

½ teaspoon kafe hawaij seasoning, or pumpkin pie spice and a pinch of black pepper

½ ounce date syrup

Ice

3 espresso beans, to garnish

TAHINI
SAUCE

EVERYTHING
BAGEL CHILI
CRISP

QUICK
MANGO
AMBA

SIMPLE
APPLESAUCE

SUMAC
HOT HONEY

SUNFLOWER
TAHINI

APPLE
AND PEAR
CHAROSET

DUKKAH

EVERYTHING
BAGEL SPICE

CHIA JAM

ZHOUG

CASHEW
CREAM
CHEESE

HOT
MUSTARD

GARLIC
TOUM

Essentials

Sauerkraut

MAKES About 2 pints

ON THE TABLE IN… 4 to 10 days, including 30 minutes to prep

Sauerkraut is an easy entry point to lactic acid fermentation because it has only two key ingredients: salt and cabbage. It has long been a staple in my kitchen, not only for its briny, tangy taste but also for its probiotic, gut-healthy benefits. I like adding caraway seeds for a classic German flavor, as well as bright shredded carrots when I'm using green cabbage. Red cabbage will yield a beautifully vibrant fuchsia sauerkraut. Like many pickle recipes, sauerkraut can be a blank canvas for flavorings. Try adding ¼ teaspoon of ground turmeric and a slice of fresh ginger, or add chopped garlic and red chili flakes. Make sure you use jars with sealable lids for storage.

1 large head red or green cabbage
2 tablespoons kosher salt
½ teaspoon caraway seeds (optional)
1 carrot, shredded (optional)

Wash and dry 2 pint-size mason jars with hot water. Set aside.

Discard the wilted outer leaves from the cabbage. Cut in half vertically and cut out the core. Cut each half into 4 wedges. Thinly shred the cabbage crosswise and place in a large bowl. Add the salt and, using your hands, massage and squeeze the salt into the cabbage until the cabbage wilts, becomes watery, and the liquid starts to collect in the bowl, 5 to 10 minutes. Don't be afraid to use force—the cabbage can take it and it should start to break down. You can use food-safe rubber gloves if you prefer or have any cuts or dry skin.

Add the caraway and/or carrot, if using.

Divide the cabbage between the 2 jars. It might seem like too much, but use your hands to tightly pack the cabbage into the jars. You are looking for liquid to seep out of the cabbage and start filling the jar. If there is any leftover liquid in the large bowl, divide it between the jars.

Leave a 1-inch gap between the cabbage and the top of the jar. You want the cabbage to be fully submerged in the liquid. If it isn't, dissolve 1 tablespoon of salt in 1 cup of water and add it to the jar until it covers the cabbage.

Weigh the cabbage down using clean stones or marbles.

Place cheesecloth or a clean kitchen towel over the jar and secure it with an elastic band. Let it sit in a cool, dark place for 24 hours.

24 hours later Press down on the cabbage using (clean) hands to submerge it into the liquid.

Ferment for at least 3 more or up to 10 days, in a cool, dark place, checking daily. Check to see whether it is ready by tasting a small piece of cabbage. Once it is to your liking, seal the jar with its lid and keep in the refrigerator.

ESSENTIALS

SAUERKRAUT SYMPTOMS

The temperature of your home can impact making sauerkraut. It will ferment more quickly in the summer than in winter, so be sure to check it periodically.

BAD

- Black scum on the top of the cabbage—if dark mold forms, skim it off and discard it. The sauerkraut itself is still okay!

GOOD

- Bubbles form in the jar
- Light or white foam at the top of the jar
- Cabbage softening

Quick Pickled Onions

MAKES 1 pint

ON THE TABLE IN… 2 hours 15 minutes, including 2 hours of resting time

I always have a jar of pickled onions in the fridge ready for topping salads, grain bowls, sandwiches, a bagel with schmear, or Carrot "Lox" (page 50). Any onion can be used, but I love the pink hue of red onions. Flavored with black pepper, fennel, and coriander, these sweet and tangy onions can also be customized with the addition of a cinnamon stick, a slice of fresh ginger, or a teaspoon of red chili flakes. Make sure you use a jar with a sealable lid for storage.

1 cup white wine vinegar or standard white vinegar
¼ cup sugar
1 tablespoon sea salt
2 teaspoons black peppercorns
1 teaspoon fennel seeds
1 teaspoon coriander seeds
2 garlic cloves, peeled
1 bay leaf
1 medium red onion, cut into half-moons

In a small saucepan over medium heat, combine the vinegar, sugar, salt, peppercorns, fennel seeds, coriander, garlic, and bay leaf and cook until it begins to bubble slightly.

Meanwhile, fill a clean jam jar or mason jar with the onion. Pour the vinegar mixture over the onion, seal, and refrigerate for at least 2 hours or overnight. The pickled onions will keep in the refrigerator for up to 1 month.

Refrigerated Pickled Everything

MAKES: **2 pints**

ON THE TABLE IN... **2 hours 15 minutes,** including 2 hours of resting time

Pickling is one of my favorite ways to use up vegetables in the back of the fridge and reduce my food waste. I've been experimenting with pickling for over a decade, testing brines, spices, and vegetables to make my perfect pickle. The classic pickles at the deli counter are typically salt-fermented and can take weeks to make, whereas this recipe is for nearly instant pickles, with whatever you have on hand! Some of my favorite vegetables to pickle in this recipe are cauliflower florets, carrots, and green beans.

1 pound fresh vegetables (green beans, carrots, cauliflower, jalapeños, radishes, or Kirby cucumbers)

4 sprigs fresh dill

1 teaspoon black peppercorns

1 teaspoon coriander seeds

4 garlic cloves, peeled and smashed

1 cup white vinegar or white wine vinegar

1 cup water

1-inch piece lemon peel

1 tablespoon salt

1 tablespoon sugar

Rinse and dry the vegetables. Cut them into uniform pieces (trim the ends of green beans, peel and slice carrots, cut cauliflower into florets, cut jalapeños into slices, halve radishes, or cut cucumbers into spears or leave whole if small).

Divide the dill, peppercorns, coriander seeds, and garlic cloves between 2 pint containers with lids. Add the vegetables to the containers, squishing them into the jar; it should be tight!

In a medium saucepan over medium heat, bring the vinegar, water, lemon peel, salt, and sugar to a boil to make a brine.

Pour the liquid brine over the vegetables to cover. The vegetables should be fully submerged.

Let the vegetables cool to room temperature. Seal with a tight-fitting lid and store in the refrigerator overnight. The vegetables will stay crisp for up to 3 weeks.

Tahini Sauce

MAKES: 1 cup

ON THE TABLE IN… 5 minutes

Tahini is one of the most used ingredients in my pantry. From Vegan Tahini Olive Oil Challah (page 205) to Smooth and Creamy Hummus, Four Ways (page 119) to Creamy Mamaliga (page 107), the rich and nutty flavor complements both sweet and savory dishes. Tahini sauce is one of my favorite ways to use this special ingredient. I like to keep a jar in the fridge to use for dressing salads, dipping vegetables, or as a creamy vegan pasta sauce.

½ cup tahini
½ cup cold water, plus more as needed
3 tablespoons lemon juice
½ teaspoon ground cumin
¼ teaspoon sea salt

In a medium bowl, whisk together the tahini, water, lemon juice, cumin, and salt. Add more water, 1 teaspoon at a time, as needed to get the consistency you want.

Store in a sealed jar in the refrigerator for up to 4 days. Tahini sauce will thicken over time, so add water as needed to thin it to the desired consistency.

Sunflower Tahini

MAKES: 2 cups

ON THE TABLE IN… 10 minutes

An alternative to sesame tahini, this version was inspired by my Ukrainian heritage and the country's national flower. In Eastern European cuisine, the halvah they use is made with sunflower seeds, because the sunflower is widely grown in that region. Sunflower tahini can be used in place of sesame tahini in hummus or tahini sauce, and it can be a great substitute when dealing with sesame allergies.

2 cups raw unsalted sunflower seeds
4 to 5 tablespoons neutral oil, such as avocado, divided
½ teaspoon sea salt

Combine the sunflower seeds, 3 tablespoons of the oil, and the salt in a blender or food processor and blend until smooth, 6 to 8 minutes. Adding the remaining 1 to 2 tablespoons of oil, as needed, to get the desired consistency.

Store the tahini in a sealed jar in the refrigerator or in a cool dark place for up to 1 month.

Zhoug

MAKES: 1 cup

ON THE TABLE IN... 10 minutes

This is a green, herbaceous, and spicy condiment of Yemeni origins. While this recipe uses cilantro and parsley, go ahead and experiment with your favorite herbs and use the often ignored and wasted stems! Add zhoug to eggs, hummus, or salad dressings or use it as a spread on your favorite sandwich.

1 cup fresh parsley, stems included
1 cup fresh cilantro, stems included
2 garlic cloves, peeled
1 small jalapeño, roughly chopped
¼ teaspoon ground cumin
¼ teaspoon ground cardamom
¼ teaspoon salt
1 tablespoon lemon juice
½ cup olive oil

Combine the parsley, cilantro, garlic, and jalapeño in a blender or food processor and pulse until finely chopped. Add the cumin, cardamom, salt, and lemon juice and pulse a few times to combine.

With the food processor or blender running, drizzle in the oil. Note: You can also make this using a mortar and pestle.

Store in an airtight container in the refrigerator for up to 1 week.

Sumac Hot Honey

MAKES: ¾ cup

ON THE TABLE IN... 20 minutes

In the last few years, hot honey has taken over and is being used in all kinds of dishes from pizzas to pancakes. I love the sweet heat that hot honey imparts on a dish, whether I'm drizzling it over roasted Brussels sprouts, serving it with grilled halloumi, or using it as a twist on Rosh Hashanah apple dipping! Try it over a grilled cheese with sliced apples or in your favorite salad dressing. Unlike your typical hot honey, this recipe uses tangy sumac and cider vinegar for an updated, complex sweetness I think you'll like.

¾ cup honey or agave syrup
1 tablespoon red chili flakes or Aleppo chili flakes
1 tablespoon ground sumac
1 tablespoon apple cider vinegar

In a small saucepan, combine the honey, chili flakes, and sumac and bring to a simmer over medium heat. Cook for 5 minutes.

Remove from the heat, add the apple cider vinegar, and stir until combined.

Cool to room temperature and transfer to a glass container with a lid. Store in a dark place for up to 3 months.

Garlic Toum

MAKES: 4 cups

ON THE TABLE IN… 20 minutes

Toum is a mayonnaise-type condiment that is completely vegan and contains just a few ingredients. It is made by blending (a lot of) garlic cloves with oil, lemon juice, and salt. Traditional toum is made using a neutral oil, such as vegetable oil, but I love using a spicy olive oil for a green-tinted toum that has a little bit of a kick. The key to toum is patience and very slowly drizzling the oil as the food processor is running. With time, it will be thick, fluffy, and whitish in color. Add toum on top of grain bowls like the Sabich Grain Bowl with Crispy Chickpeas (page 158), falafel wraps, sandwiches, or eggs.

1 cup garlic cloves, peeled
 (about 8 small or 4 large heads)
2 teaspoons sea salt
3 cups olive oil, divided
½ cup lemon juice, divided

Place the garlic cloves and salt in a food processor and pulse until the garlic is very finely minced, scraping down the sides of the food processor as needed.

With the food processor running, slowly drizzle 1 cup of the oil into the garlic, then alternate with 1 to 2 tablespoons of the lemon juice. Continue alternating with another cup of oil and then lemon juice, until it has all been added. This should be done very slowly for it to emulsify properly, 10 to 15 minutes.

Transfer the toum to an airtight container and refrigerate for up to 3 months.

Cashew "Cream Cheese"

MAKES: 1½ cups

ON THE TABLE IN… 15 minutes

There's no bagel without schmear—and if you are plant-based, dairy-free, or lactose intolerant, many vegan cream cheeses leave a lot to be desired. Making your own couldn't be easier. The trick to making vegan cream cheese is miso, a savory, salty, and umami-rich soy-based ingredient. Spread this "cream cheese" over Mini Montreal Bagels (page 218) or on a piece of matzo during Passover.

2 cups raw cashews
¾ cup water, plus more for soaking
2 tablespoons lemon juice
1 teaspoon apple cider vinegar
1½ teaspoons miso paste
¼ teaspoon salt

In a medium bowl, soak the cashews in hot water for 5 to 10 minutes. Drain and rinse in a colander.

In a blender or food processor, combine the soaked cashews, ¾ cup of water, lemon juice, vinegar, miso, and salt and blend until smooth.

Transfer to an airtight container and refrigerate for up to 1 week or freeze for up to 3 months.

ESSENTIALS

Manischewitz Blueberry Compote

MAKES: 2 cups

ON THE TABLE IN... 20 minutes

My zaida (grandfather) Arnold had a soft spot for sweet kosher wine, which tastes like grape juice with a slight alcohol aftertaste. It was so ingrained in our family that no holiday was complete without two bottles of Manischewitz—one bottle for the adults' table and one for the kids' table. We would sip a thimbleful of the wine during Passover and at Friday-night dinners, cheering l'chaim ("to life") at celebrations. For me, Manischewitz wine means family. This compote plays on the sweetness of this kosher fruit wine as it simmers with juicy blueberries and lemon, creating a not-too-sweet sauce that complements blintzes, pancakes, waffles, oatmeal, and even cheesecake.

4 cups frozen blueberries

¾ cup + 2 tablespoons sweet kosher wine, such as Manischewitz, divided

1 (1-inch) piece lemon peel

2 tablespoons lemon juice

Pinch sea salt

2 teaspoons cornstarch or potato starch

Combine the frozen blueberries, ¾ cup of the wine, lemon peel, lemon juice, and salt in a medium saucepan over medium heat and bring to a boil. Decrease the heat to medium-low and simmer until the blueberries start to break down, 12 to 15 minutes. Use a fork or potato masher to mash the blueberries slightly.

Meanwhile, in a small bowl, use a fork to whisk the remaining 2 tablespoons of wine and cornstarch to make a slurry. Add the cornstarch slurry to the saucepan and stir vigorously until thickened.

Serve immediately or transfer to a heat-safe container. The compote will thicken slightly as it cools.

NOTE: Compote will keep in a covered container in the fridge for up to 4 days.

VARIATION: For a more classic compote, use Concord grape juice in place of wine. If seasonal, substitute equal amounts of fresh blueberries for frozen.

WHAT IS MANISCHEWITZ WINE? Manischewitz is a kosher wine known for being syrupy sweet. It was created in response to a growing Jewish population in the United States during the 1940s. Grapes were sourced from Upstate New York, which meant that it was close enough to the winemaking facility (in Brooklyn) to undergo rabbinical supervision, but it also meant that the grapes were of lesser quality. This prompted the winemakers to add sugar to the mix, giving it a flavor somewhere between wine and Concord grape juice. Manischewitz wine was largely known only by the Jewish population until the 1960s, when Sammy Davis Jr. starred in a commercial, "Man, Oh Manischewitz," which became a viral hit.

Chia Raspberry Jam

MAKES: 1½ cups

ON THE TABLE IN... 20 minutes

As a child, my sister and I would visit my grandparents in Vancouver every summer. We would go berry picking and make a sticky-sweet jam using our bounty in my grandmother's kitchen, taking turns dumping in cups of sugar and stirring the pot with a large wooden spoon. We'd lick our fingers and have jam and margarine sandwiches for lunch before canning. It was an early introduction to the kitchen and a memory that has always stuck with me. This is my modern take on my grandmother's raspberry jam, made in 20 minutes or less, using modern (and nutritious!) ingredients.

2 cups frozen raspberries
1 tablespoon lemon juice
2 tablespoons chia seeds
1 tablespoon maple syrup

In a saucepan over medium heat, cook the raspberries until warmed through, using a fork or potato masher to break them down further.

Add the lemon juice, chia seeds, and maple syrup and stir to combine.

Remove from the heat and let sit until it begins to thicken, about 10 minutes. The jam will continue to thicken over time.

Transfer the jam to a sealed jar or container and refrigerate for up to 1 week.

Apple and Pear Charoset

MAKES: About 4 cups

ON THE TABLE IN... 20 minutes

Charoset has always been a highlight of Passover. Charoset recipes vary depending on culture and location, but they are typically made of fresh or dried fruits, nuts, spices, wine, and honey. Charoset comes from the Hebrew word for clay, cheres, and represents the mortar used by the Jewish people when enslaved in Egypt. In my family, charoset was not limited to the seder plate, but was eaten with yogurt, on top of matzo, or on its own throughout the Passover holiday.

1 Granny Smith apple, peeled, cored, and cut into ¼-inch pieces
1 medium green pear, unpeeled, cut into ¼-inch pieces
2 teaspoons ground cinnamon
1½ teaspoons ground ginger
½ teaspoon orange zest
¼ teaspoon ground cardamom (optional)
⅓ cup sweet red wine
1 cup walnuts, finely chopped
½ cup pitted dates, finely chopped
1 tablespoon maple syrup (optional)

Combine the apples and pears in a bowl. Add the cinnamon, ginger, orange zest, cardamom (if using), red wine, walnuts, and dates and mix until combined. Stir in the maple syrup, if you prefer a sweeter charoset. Let sit for 10 minutes.

Hot Mustard

MAKES: ½ cup

ON THE TABLE IN... 10 minutes

My grandpa Louis wasn't often in the kitchen, but when he was, he would be mixing up a bowl of his famous hot mustard to serve with brisket. I never knew how easy it was until years later when I got my hands on his secret recipe. If you've never thought about making your own mustard, let this spicy mustard be your introduction to DIY condiments.

6 tablespoons mustard powder (such as Colman's)
3 tablespoons white vinegar
4 teaspoons honey or maple syrup
½ teaspoon sea salt
⅛ teaspoon ground turmeric
3 to 5 tablespoons cold water

In a small bowl, whisk together the mustard powder, vinegar, honey, salt, and turmeric. Add 3 tablespoons of the water and whisk until combined. Let sit for 10 minutes before serving. It will thicken slightly as it sets, so add 1½ teaspoons of water at a time, as needed, to adjust the consistency.

Store in the fridge for up to 1 week.

Dukkah

MAKES: 1 cup

ON THE TABLE IN... 10 minutes

Try this nutty spice blend in the Dukkah-Crusted Fried Cauliflower "Steaks" (page 148).

1 cup raw hazelnuts
2 tablespoons cumin seeds
2 tablespoons fennel seeds
¼ cup coriander seeds
¼ cup unsalted pumpkin seeds
3 tablespoons sesame seeds
1 teaspoon kosher salt

Place the hazelnuts in a food processor and pulse a few times to break them into pebble-size pieces. Add the cumin, fennel, and coriander seeds and pulse to break them into smaller pieces. Add the pumpkin and sesame seeds and pulse until the mixture has broken down into very small pieces, similar to sesame seeds or sunflower seeds.

Transfer the nuts and seeds to a skillet set over medium heat and toast until fragrant, 3 to 5 minutes. Add the salt.

Transfer to an airtight container and store in the cupboard for up to 3 months.

KITNIYOT-FREE DUKKAH VARIATION

1 cup hazelnuts
¼ cup pumpkin seeds
1 tablespoons red chili flakes
1 teaspoon ground cinnamon
1 tablespoon garlic granules

2 teaspoons dried mint
1 teaspoon kosher salt
Pulse all the ingredients in a food processor until very small. Then follow the instructions in the main recipe.

Quick Mango Amba

MAKES: ¾ cup

ON THE TABLE IN... 20 minutes

Amba is a sweet, savory, and tart mango condiment common in Indian, Iraqi, and Israeli cuisine. In India it is made using pickled mangoes and mustard oil, whereas Iraqi versions usually use a ripe mango and do not add mustard oil. This recipe relies on frozen mango and a combination of herbs, spices, and vinegar to replicate the flavor of traditional amba in just 20 minutes.

1½ cups frozen mango, defrosted
2 garlic cloves, peeled
¼ cup water
⅓ cup apple cider vinegar
½ teaspoon ground fenugreek
½ teaspoon ground cumin
¼ teaspoon red chili flakes
1 tablespoon maple syrup or honey
¼ teaspoon salt

In a blender or food processor, combine the mango, garlic, water, apple cider vinegar, fenugreek, cumin, chili flakes, maple syrup, and salt and blend until smooth.

Pour the mango mixture into a small saucepan and bring to a boil over medium heat. Once boiling, lower the heat and simmer until thickened, 10 to 15 minutes.

Transfer to an airtight container and store in the fridge for up to 2 weeks.

Shawarma Spice Blend

MAKES: About ½ cup

ON THE TABLE IN... 5 minutes

Make this flavorful spice blend in advance and store it in the pantry. Try tossing cauliflower florets in olive oil and this spice blend before roasting, add it to sweet potato fries, or blend a teaspoon into your hummus.

3 tablespoons ground cumin
2 tablespoons sweet paprika
2 teaspoons ground coriander
1 teaspoon ground turmeric
1 teaspoon ground ginger
1 teaspoon garlic powder
½ teaspoon ground cinnamon
½ teaspoon ground cardamom
½ teaspoon sea salt
¼ teaspoon red chili flakes

Combine all the ingredients in a jar with a lid and store in the cupboard for up to 6 months.

Simple Applesauce

MAKES: 2 cups

ON THE TABLE IN… 25 minutes

During Hanukkah, we would always make our own homemade applesauce, and it was the highlight of wintertime breakfast over the course of the eight days of celebration. Making your own couldn't be easier, I love that you can customize it entirely, adding as much or as little sugar, flavorings, and textures as you like.

4 medium apples (I like to use Granny Smith)

¾ cup water

½ teaspoon ground cinnamon

OPTIONAL

¼ cup sugar

½ teaspoons freshly grated ginger

1 pod star anise

1 teaspoon vanilla extract

Peel the apples, if you prefer. Core and roughly chop them. If keeping the peels on, use an immersion blender until smooth.

Combine the apples, water, and cinnamon in a saucepan. Add the sugar and any additional spices, if using. Cover and cook over medium heat until softened, 15 to 20 minutes.

Let cool. Mash with a potato masher or fork, or blend with an immersion blender.

Store in an airtight container in the refrigerator for up to 5 days.

Everything Bagel Chili Crisp

MAKES: 1 cup

ON THE TABLE IN… 40 minutes

Chili crisp is a type of hot oil condiment with roots in Chinese cuisine. Wildly popular on store shelves recently, it is made by frying chili peppers and other aromatic ingredients, like garlic, Sichuan pepper, nuts, and seeds, into an infused oil. I turned my favorite seasoning blend, Everything Bagel Spice (page 246), into a sweet, salty, spicy, and aromatic "good on everything" condiment. Try adding it to salads, eggs, avocado toast, bagels, or fried tofu.

1 cup neutral oil, such as grapeseed or avocado

3 red chili peppers, thinly sliced

4 garlic cloves, thinly sliced

¼ cup Everything Bagel Spice (page 246)

1 tablespoon red chili flakes

1 teaspoon sugar

1 teaspoon soy sauce, or gluten-free tamari, if preferred

In a medium saucepan over medium-low heat, combine the oil, chili peppers, and garlic. Simmer until the garlic is browned, 20 to 30 minutes.

Remove from the heat and let sit for 2 to 3 minutes.

Combine the everything bagel spice, red chili flakes, sugar, and soy sauce in a heatproof bowl. Pour the hot oil over the top and stir until combined.

Transfer to an airtight container and refrigerate for up to 2 weeks. Stir before serving.

Everything Bagel Spice

MAKES: 1¼ cups

ON THE TABLE IN... 5 minutes

Everything bagel spice goes well with…just about everything! In classic Montreal bagel bakeries, it is often called "all-dressed." Whatever you call it, it is undeniably addictive as a topping for avocado toast, salad, latkes, bagels, or challah. It was likely invented by accident by combining all the available bagel toppings and coating a bagel with it, but there's no doubt that it was a happy mistake. This recipe gives options for adding your own flair with caraway, fennel, or dried dill, making it even better than store-bought versions!

¼ cup dried minced garlic

¼ cup dried onion flakes

½ cup sesame seeds

3 tablespoons poppy seeds

4 teaspoons coarse or flaky sea salt

Combine all the ingredients in an airtight container. Store in a cool, dark place for up to 3 months.

> **VARIATIONS:** For even more flavor and spice, try adding one (or all) or the following:
> - 1 tablespoon caraway seeds
> - 2 teaspoons fennel seeds
> - 1 teaspoon dried dill

Index

A

almond flour
  Almond Flour Crepes, 67
  making, 67
  Passover Black and White
    Cookies, 180–81
  Passover-Friendly All-Year
    Pancakes, 64
almonds
  Coconut Almond Challah, 211
  Herbed Horseradish Salad, 91
  Matzo Olive Oil Granola, 63
  Moroccan-Spiced Roasted Carrot
    and Chickpea Salad, 92
amba, 36
  Quick Mango Amba, 244
appetizing, 36
apples
  Apple and Honey Porridge Bowl,
    54
  Apple and Honey Whiskey Sour,
    227
  Apple and Pear Charoset, 242
  Aunty Ethel's Jammy Apple Cake,
    198
  honey and, 199
  Salted Honey Apple Fritters,
    193–94
  -sauce, as egg substitute, 22
  Simple Applesauce, 245
aquafaba, 22
Artichoke "Marbella," Tempeh and,
  129
Ashkenazi Jews, 36
Aunty Ethel's Jammy Apple Cake,
  198

B

Baba Ghanoush, Beet, with
  Pomegranate, 116
babka, 204
  Halvah Pistachio Babka Rolls,
    202–4
bagels
  Everything Bagel "Fattoush"
    Salad with Za'atar Cheeseballs,
    88
  Mini Montreal Bagels, 215–17
  Montreal vs. New York, 216
  See also Everything Bagel Spice
baking
  high-altitude, 41
  tips for, 43
baking powder, 27

baking soda
  Passover and, 27
  vinegar and, as egg substitute, 24
bananas, mashed, as egg substitute,
  22
barley
  Sabich Grain Bowl with Crispy
    Chickpeas, 158–59
  Tempeh and Bean Cholent, 155
beans
  canned, 41–42
  Confit Tomato, Garlic, and White
    Beans with Zhoug, 174
  Heart of Palm "Whitefish" Salad,
    51
  Jackfruit and White Bean
    "Shawarma," 125
  nutrition and, 18, 20
  soaking, 20
  Tempeh and Bean Cholent, 155
  See also chickpeas
beets
  Beet and Sumac Salad with
    Oranges, 95
  Beet Baba Ghanoush with
    Pomegranate, 116
  Celeriac "Pastrami" Sandwich,
    163–64
  Fennel and Beet Borscht, 73
  greens, 148
  Red Wine–Braised Beets with
    Creamy Mamaliga, 144
bissel (bisl), definition of, 36
Black and White Cookies, Passover,
  180–81
blintzes, 36, 58
  Lemony Blintzes, 56–57
Bloody Mary, Horseradish, 228
Blueberry Compote, Manischewitz,
  241
borscht, 72
  Fennel and Beet Borscht, 73
bread
  determining doneness of, 41
  See also babka; bagels; challah;
    malawach; matzo; pita bread;
    sandwiches
"Brisket," Savory Pulled Mushroom
  and Tofu, 122
buckwheat. See kasha
buckwheat honey, 196
  Buckwheat Honey Cake, 197
buttermilk, vegan, 21
butter substitutes, 21

C

cabbage, 75
  Fennel and Beet Borscht, 73
  Kasha and Mushroom Cabbage
    Rolls, 133–35
  Sweet and Sour Cabbage Soup, 74
  See also sauerkraut
cakes
  Aunty Ethel's Jammy Apple Cake,
    198
  Buckwheat Honey Cake, 197
  Mini Halvah Cakes, 187
  Olive Oil, Pistachio, and Ricotta
    Cornmeal Sheet Cake, 201
carrots
  Carrot and Parsnip Tzimmes with
    Dates and Pecans, 108
  Carrot "Lox," 50
  Moroccan-Spiced Roasted Carrot
    and Chickpea Salad, 92
cashews
  Cashew "Cream Cheese," 240
  Funfetti Hamantaschen, 184–86
  Halvah Granola, 60
  Lemony Blintzes, 56–57
  Matzo Olive Oil Granola, 63
  Vegan "Gefilte" Cakes, 147
cauliflower
  Dukkah-Crusted Fried
    Cauliflower "Steaks," 148
  Spiced Cauliflower Chraime, 143
  Vegan "Gefilte" Cakes, 147
celeriac, 162
  Celeriac "Pastrami" Sandwich,
    163–64
Chag Sameach, 36
challah
  Cinnamon Toast Challah, 211
  Classic One-Bowl Challah,
    208–11
  Coconut Almond Challah, 211
  Everything Bagel Challah, 211
  Pizza Challah, 211
  shaping, 211
  tips for making, 207
  Unicorn Challah, 211
  Vegan Tahini Olive Oil Challah,
    205–7
chametz, 27, 36
charoset (haroset), 36
  Apple and Pear Charoset, 242
cheese
  Cashew "Cream Cheese," 240
  Celeriac "Pastrami" Sandwich,
    163–64
  Cheesy Jumbo Stuffed Kasha and
    Shells, 138–39

Everything Bagel "Fattoush" Salad with Za'atar Cheeseballs, 88
Olive Oil, Pistachio, and Ricotta Cornmeal Sheet Cake, 201
Pizza Challah, 211
Salted Chocolate Rugelach, 188–89
Sweet and Spicy Harissa Hasselback Squash with Chickpeas, 165–66
Tahini Mac and Cheese Noodle Kugel, 136
Za'atar and Feta Khachapuri, 170–71
chia seeds
Chia Raspberry Jam, 242
as egg substitute, 22
Halvah Granola, 60
Matzo Olive Oil Granola, 63
Passover and, 27
chickpeas
Baked Herby Falafel Balls, 151
Chickpea and Olive Shakshuka, 169
Chickpea Noodle Vegetable Soup, 70
Moroccan-Spiced Roasted Carrot and Chickpea Salad, 92
Olive, Chickpea, and Zucchini Stew with Preserved Lemons, 156
Sabich Grain Bowl with Crispy Chickpeas, 158–59
Smooth and Creamy Hummus, Four Ways, 119
Sweet and Spicy Harissa Hasselback Squash with Chickpeas, 165–66
Tempeh and Bean Cholent, 155
Chili Crisp, Everything Bagel, 245
chocolate
Kitchen Sink Mandelbrot, 178
melting, 42
Passover Black and White Cookies, 180–81
Passover Coconut Macaroons, 182–83
Salted Chocolate Rugelach, 188–89
cholent, 36, 155
Tempeh and Bean Cholent, 155
chraime, 36, 142
Spiced Cauliflower Chraime, 143
cilantro
Baked Herby Falafel Balls, 151
Crispy Tahdig Rice "Latkes," 105–6

Olive, Chickpea, and Zucchini Stew with Preserved Lemons, 156
Spiced Cauliflower Chraime, 143
Zhoug, 239
cinnamon
Cinnamon Matzo, 222
Cinnamon Toast Challah, 211
coconut
Coconut Almond Challah, 211
Halvah Granola, 60
Kitchen Sink Mandelbrot, 178
Matzo Olive Oil Granola, 63
Passover Coconut Macaroons, 182–83
coconut cream, 114
Pumpkin Kugel with Pecan Streusel, 115
coconut milk
Fennel and Beet Borscht, 73
Malabi Porridge with Rose Essence, Pomegranate, and Pistachio, 53
Passover Coconut Macaroons, 182–83
confit, 175
Confit Tomato, Garlic, and White Beans with Zhoug, 174
cookies
Funfetti Hamantaschen, 184–86
Kitchen Sink Mandelbrot, 178
Mohn (Poppy Seed) Cookies, 179
Passover Black and White Cookies, 180–81
Passover Coconut Macaroons, 182–83
Salted Chocolate Rugelach, 188–89
Cornmeal Sheet Cake, Olive Oil, Pistachio, and Ricotta, 201
cream
substitutes for, 21
Whipped Cream, 201
crepes
Almond Flour Crepes, 67
See also blintzes
cucumbers
Crispy Tahdig Rice "Latkes," 105–6
Everything Bagel "Fattoush" Salad with Za'atar Cheeseballs, 88
Herbed Horseradish Salad, 91
Pomegranate Lentil Tabbouleh, 99
Sabich Grain Bowl with Crispy Chickpeas, 158–59
Smashed Cucumber Dill Salad, 96

D
dairy substitutes, 20–22
dates
Apple and Pear Charoset, 242
Carrot and Parsnip Tzimmes with Dates and Pecans, 108
Date Syrup and Hawaij Espresso Martini, 231
Tempeh and Bean Cholent, 155
Diaspora, definition of, 36
donuts
Classic Yeasted Sufganiyot, 191–92
Salted Honey Apple Fritters, 193–94
drinks
Apple and Honey Whiskey Sour, 227
Date Syrup and Hawaij Espresso Martini, 231
Halvah Milkshake, 230
Horseradish Bloody Mary, 228
Mulled Manischewitz, 229
New York Sour with Red Wine and Pomegranate Molasses, 229
Olive and Sumac Martini, 227
Pomegranate Red Wine Spritzer, 226
Vegan Egg Cream, 230
dukkah (duqqa), 36–37, 145
Dukkah-Crusted Fried Cauliflower "Steaks," 148
making, 243
dumplings
names for, 132
Poppy Seed, Potato, and Caramelized Onion Kreplach, 78–80
Sweet Potato and Sage Vareniki with Hazelnuts, 130–32

E
eggplant
Beet Baba Ghanoush with Pomegranate, 116
Sabich Grain Bowl with Crispy Chickpeas, 158–59
eggs
Sabich Grain Bowl with Crispy Chickpeas, 158–59
substitutes for, 22, 24
Vegan Egg Cream, 230
Espresso Martini, Date Syrup and Hawaij, 231
Everything Bagel Spice, 246
Everything Bagel Challah, 211

Everything Bagel Chili Crisp, 245
Everything Bagel "Fattoush" Salad with Za'atar Cheeseballs, 88
Israeli Everything Pita Bread, 212–14
Mini Montreal Bagels, 215–17
Smooth and Creamy Hummus, Four Ways, 119

F
falafel, 150
Baked Herby Falafel Balls, 151
fattoush
Everything Bagel "Fattoush" Salad with Za'atar Cheeseballs, 88
Israeli salad vs., 89
Fennel and Beet Borscht, 73
flax seeds
as egg substitute, 22, 24
Kasha and Mushroom Cabbage Rolls, 133–35
Kitchen Sink Mandelbrot, 178
Matzo Olive Oil Granola, 63
Passover and, 27
Floater Herbed Matzo Balls, 85
flour, measuring, 41
food waste, reducing, 42–43
Fritters, Salted Honey Apple, 193–94
fruits, dried
Halvah Granola, 60
Matzo Olive Oil Granola, 63
frying tips, 192
Funfetti Hamantaschen, 184–86

G
garlic
Confit Tomato, Garlic, and White Beans with Zhoug, 174
Everything Bagel Spice, 246
Garlic and Herb Matzo, 222
Garlic Toum, 240
gefilte, 147
Vegan "Gefilte" Cakes, 147
gin
Olive and Sumac Martini, 227
goulash, 37
Hearty Lentil Goulash, 152
grains
as protein source, 18
See also individual grains
granola
Halvah Granola, 60
Matzo Olive Oil Granola, 63

H
halvah, 37
Halvah Granola, 60
Halvah Milkshake, 230
Halvah Pistachio Babka Rolls, 202–4
Mini Halvah Cakes, 187
Hamantaschen, Funfetti, 184–86
Hanukkah, 31, 38, 100, 105, 122, 191, 193, 245
harissa, 37, 166
Smooth and Creamy Hummus, Four Ways, 119
Sweet and Spicy Harissa Hasselback Squash with Chickpeas, 165–66
hazelnuts
Dukkah, 243
Sweet Potato and Sage Vareniki with Hazelnuts, 130–32
herbs
Baked Herby Falafel Balls, 151
Floater Herbed Matzo Balls, 85
Garlic and Herb Matzo, 222
Herbed Horseradish Salad, 91
storing fresh, 42
See also individual herbs
honey
Apple and Honey Porridge Bowl, 54
Apple and Honey Whiskey Sour, 227
apples and, 199
buckwheat, 196
Buckwheat Honey Cake, 197
Salted Honey Apple Fritters, 193–94
Sumac Hot Honey, 239
vegan alternatives to, 194
horseradish
Herbed Horseradish Salad, 91
Horseradish Bloody Mary, 228
Passover and, 90
hummus
secret to creamy, 118
Smooth and Creamy Hummus, Four Ways, 119

I
ice cream
Halvah Milkshake, 230
iron, 19–20
Israeli Everything Pita Bread, 212–14

J
Jackfruit and White Bean "Shawarma," 125
jams and jellies
Aunty Ethel's Jammy Apple Cake, 198
Chia Raspberry Jam, 242
Classic Yeasted Sufganiyot, 191–92

K
Kahlúa
Date Syrup and Hawaij Espresso Martini, 231
kasha, 37, 139
Cheesy Jumbo Stuffed Kasha and Shells, 138–39
Kasha and Mushroom Cabbage Rolls, 133–35
khachapuri, 171
Za'atar and Feta Khachapuri, 170–71
Kitchen Sink Mandelbrot, 178
kitniyot, 27
kreplach, 37
Poppy Seed, Potato, and Caramelized Onion Kreplach, 78–80
kugel, 37, 137
Cast-Iron Potato and Caramelized Onion Kugel, 110–11
Pumpkin Kugel with Pecan Streusel, 115
Tahini Mac and Cheese Noodle Kugel, 136

L
labneh, 37
latkes
Crispy Tahdig Rice "Latkes," 105–6
making crispy, 101
Vegan Potato Latkes, 100–101
lemons
Lemony Blintzes, 56–57
Olive, Chickpea, and Zucchini Stew with Preserved Lemons, 156
preserved, 157
Yossi's Lemony Lentil Soup, 77
lentils, 76
Hearty Lentil Goulash, 152
Pomegranate Lentil Tabbouleh, 99
Yossi's Lemony Lentil Soup, 77
liquid smoke, 50

lox, 37
  Carrot "Lox," 50

M

macaroons
  macarons vs., 183
  Passover Coconut Macaroons,
    182–83
malabi, 37, 52
  Malabi Porridge with Rose
    Essence, Pomegranate, and
    Pistachio, 53
malawach, 37, 219
  Sesame Seed Malawach, 218–19
mamaliga, 37, 107
  Creamy Mamaliga, 107
  Red Wine–Braised Beets with
    Creamy Mamaliga, 144
mandelbrot, 37–38
  Kitchen Sink Mandelbrot, 178
Mango Amba, Quick, 244
Manischewitz. See wine
"Marbella," Tempeh and Artichoke,
  129
martinis
  Date Syrup and Hawaij Espresso
    Martini, 231
  Olive and Sumac Martini, 227
matzo, 27, 223
  brei, 38
  Cinnamon Matzo, 222
  farfel, 62
  Garlic and Herb Matzo, 222
  Homemade Matzo, 222
  Matzo Olive Oil Granola, 63
  Turmeric Matzo, 222
matzo balls
  Floater Herbed Matzo Balls, 85
  freezing, 85
  Turmeric Vegetable Matzo Ball
    Soup, 83
  Vegan Matzo Balls, 84
matzo meal
  Cast-Iron Potato and
    Caramelized Onion Kugel,
    110–11
  Dukkah-Crusted Fried
    Cauliflower "Steaks," 148
  Vegan "Gefilte" Cakes, 147
  See also matzo balls
measuring, 41
meat alternatives, 18
menus, 31–32
milk
  Halvah Milkshake, 230
  substitutes for, 20–21, 41
miso, 71

Mizrahi Jews, 38
Mohn (Poppy Seed) Cookies, 179
Montreal Bagels, Mini, 215–17
Moroccan-Spiced Roasted Carrot
  and Chickpea Salad, 92
mushrooms
  Cheesy Jumbo Stuffed Kasha and
    Shells, 138–39
  Kasha and Mushroom Cabbage
    Rolls, 133–35
  protein and, 123
  Savory Pulled Mushroom and
    Tofu "Brisket," 122
Mustard, Hot, 243

N

New York Sour with Red Wine and
  Pomegranate Molasses, 229
noodles. See pasta and noodles
nosh, definition of, 38
nut butters, 43
nuts, 19, 20. See also individual nuts

O

oats
  Apple and Honey Porridge Bowl,
    54
  Halvah Granola, 60
olive oil
  choosing, 43
  Matzo Olive Oil Granola, 63
  Olive Oil, Pistachio, and Ricotta
    Cornmeal Sheet Cake, 201
  Vegan Tahini Olive Oil Challah,
    205–7
olives
  Chickpea and Olive Shakshuka,
    169
  Olive and Sumac Martini, 227
  Olive, Chickpea, and Zucchini
    Stew with Preserved Lemons,
    156
  Tempeh and Artichoke
    "Marbella," 129
onions
  caramelizing, 111
  Cast-Iron Potato and
    Caramelized Onion Kugel,
    110–11
  Everything Bagel Spice, 246
  Poppy Seed, Potato, and
    Caramelized Onion Kreplach,
    78–80
  Quick Pickled Onions, 235
  tempering sharp-flavored, 93
Oranges, Beet and Sumac Salad
  with, 95

P

palm, hearts of, 51
  Heart of Palm "Whitefish" Salad,
    51
Pancakes, Passover-Friendly All-
  Year, 64
paprika, 153
pareve, 38
parsley
  Baked Herby Falafel Balls, 151
  Everything Bagel "Fattoush"
    Salad with Za'atar Cheeseballs,
    88
  Pomegranate Lentil Tabbouleh,
    99
  Zhoug, 239
parsnips
  Carrot and Parsnip Tzimmes with
    Dates and Pecans, 108
  Vegan "Gefilte" Cakes, 147
Passover
  food for, 63, 64, 67, 83, 91, 143,
    180–83, 242
  horseradish and, 90
  keeping kosher for, 27
  matzo for, 223
  seder menu, 31
pasta and noodles
  Cheesy Jumbo Stuffed Kasha and
    Shells, 138–39
  Chickpea Noodle Vegetable Soup,
    70
  Tahini Mac and Cheese Noodle
    Kugel, 136
"Pastrami" Sandwich, Celeriac,
  163–64
peanuts
  Kitchen Sink Mandelbrot, 178
Pear Charoset, Apple and, 242
pecans
  Carrot and Parsnip Tzimmes with
    Dates and Pecans, 108
  Pumpkin Kugel with Pecan
    Streusel, 115
peppers
  Chickpea and Olive Shakshuka,
    169
  Hearty Lentil Goulash, 152
  Smooth and Creamy Hummus,
    Four Ways, 119
pickles, 97
  Quick Pickled Onions, 235
  Refrigerated Pickled Everything,
    236
pistachios
  Beet and Sumac Salad with
    Oranges, 95

Crispy Tahdig Rice "Latkes," 105–6
Halvah Granola, 60
Halvah Pistachio Babka Rolls,
    202–4
Malabi Porridge with Rose
    Essence, Pomegranate, and
    Pistachio, 53
Olive Oil, Pistachio, and Ricotta
    Cornmeal Sheet Cake, 201
pita bread
    Israeli Everything Pita Bread,
        212–14
    Israeli-style, 214
Pizza Challah, 211
polenta
    Creamy Mamaliga, 107
pomegranate molasses, 117
    New York Sour with Red Wine
        and Pomegranate Molasses,
        229
pomegranates, 98
    Beet Baba Ghanoush with
        Pomegranate, 116
    Malabi Porridge with Rose
        Essence, Pomegranate, and
        Pistachio, 53
    Pomegranate Lentil Tabbouleh,
        99
    Pomegranate Red Wine Spritzer,
        226
poppy seeds, 179
    Everything Bagel Spice, 246
    Mini Montreal Bagels, 215–17
    Mohn (Poppy Seed) Cookies, 179
    Poppy Seed, Potato, and
        Caramelized Onion Kreplach,
        78–80
porridge
    Apple and Honey Porridge Bowl,
        54
    Creamy Mamaliga, 107
    Malabi Porridge with Rose
        Essence, Pomegranate, and
        Pistachio, 53
potato chips
    Kitchen Sink Mandelbrot, 178
potatoes
    Cast-Iron Potato and
        Caramelized Onion Kugel,
        110–11
    Fennel and Beet Borscht, 73
    Hearty Lentil Goulash, 152
    Poppy Seed, Potato, and
        Caramelized Onion Kreplach,
        78–80
    Vegan "Gefilte" Cakes, 147
    Vegan Potato Latkes, 100–101

pretzels
    Kitchen Sink Mandelbrot, 178
protein, 18–19
pumpkin puree
    as egg substitute, 22
    Pumpkin Kugel with Pecan
        Streusel, 115
pumpkin seeds
    Dukkah, 243
    Sweet and Spicy Harissa
        Hasselback Squash with
        Chickpeas, 165–66
Purim, 184, 186

R
radicchio
    Herbed Horseradish Salad, 91
rainbow sprinkles
    Funfetti Hamantaschen, 184–86
    Unicorn Challah, 211
Raspberry Jam, Chia, 242
recipes, halving or doubling, 42
rice
    Crispy Tahdig Rice "Latkes," 105–6
    Malabi Porridge with Rose
        Essence, Pomegranate, and
        Pistachio, 53
    Yossi's Lemony Lentil Soup, 77
Rolls, Halvah Pistachio Babka,
    202–4
Rosh Hashanah, 31, 36, 54, 55, 98,
    129, 137, 142, 143, 193, 197, 227, 239
rugelach, 189
    Salted Chocolate Rugelach,
        188–89

S
sabich, 38, 159
    Sabich Grain Bowl with Crispy
        Chickpeas, 158–59
salads
    Beet and Sumac Salad with
        Oranges, 95
    Everything Bagel "Fattoush"
        Salad with Za'atar Cheeseballs,
        88
    Heart of Palm "Whitefish" Salad,
        51
    Herbed Horseradish Salad, 91
    Israeli vs. fattoush, 89
    Moroccan-Spiced Roasted Carrot
        and Chickpea Salad, 92
    Pomegranate Lentil Tabbouleh,
        99
    Smashed Cucumber Dill Salad, 96
salt, 42, 43

sandwiches
    Celeriac "Pastrami" Sandwich,
        163–64
    sabich, 159
sauces
    Simple Applesauce, 245
    Tahini Sauce, 238
sauerkraut
    making, 234–35
    Sweet and Sour Cabbage Soup, 74
schmear, 38
schnitzel, 38, 127
    Sesame Tofu "Schnitzel," 126
seder, 31, 38, 90, 91, 242
seeds, 19, 20. See also individual seeds
seitan, 19
Sephardic (Sephardi) Jews, 38
sesame seeds
    Dukkah, 243
    Everything Bagel Spice, 246
    Halvah Granola, 60
    Mini Montreal Bagels, 215–17
    Pomegranate Lentil Tabbouleh,
        99
    Sabich Grain Bowl with Crispy
        Chickpeas, 158–59
    Sesame Seed Malawach, 218–19
    Sesame Tofu "Schnitzel," 126
Shabbat
    dinner menus, 32
    food for, 37, 78, 115, 137, 142, 143,
        147, 156, 159, 204, 205, 208, 226,
        229
    matrix, 28
shakshuka, 168
    Chickpea and Olive Shakshuka,
        169
Shavuot, 52, 58, 201
shawarma
    Jackfruit and White Bean
        "Shawarma," 125
    Shawarma Spice Blend, 244
Simchat Torah, 135
soups
    Chickpea Noodle Vegetable Soup,
        70
    Fennel and Beet Borscht, 73
    fixing salty, 84
    Sweet and Sour Cabbage Soup, 74
    Turmeric Vegetable Matzo Ball
        Soup, 83
    Yossi's Lemony Lentil Soup, 77
sour cream, vegan, 22
squash
    Olive, Chickpea, and Zucchini
        Stew with Preserved Lemons,
        156

Sweet and Spicy Harissa
    Hasselback Squash with
    Chickpeas, 165–66
sufganiyot, 38
    Classic Yeasted Sufganiyot,
    191–92
Sukkot, 115, 135, 137
sumac, 38, 94
    Beet and Sumac Salad with
    Oranges, 95
    Olive and Sumac Martini, 227
    Sumac Hot Honey, 239
sunflower seeds
    Sunflower Tahini, 238
    Tamari Sunflower Seeds, 174
sweet potatoes
    Carrot and Parsnip Tzimmes with
    Dates and Pecans, 108
    Sweet and Sour Cabbage Soup, 74
    Sweet Potato and Sage Vareniki
    with Hazelnuts, 130–32
    Tempeh and Bean Cholent, 155

T

Tabbouleh, Pomegranate Lentil, 99
tahdig, 106
    Crispy Tahdig Rice "Latkes,"
    105–6
tahini, 38
    Halvah Granola, 60
    Mini Halvah Cakes, 187
    Sabich Grain Bowl with Crispy
    Chickpeas, 158–59
    Smooth and Creamy Hummus,
    Four Ways, 119
    Sunflower Tahini, 238
    Tahini Mac and Cheese Noodle
    Kugel, 136
    Tahini Sauce, 238
    Vegan Tahini Olive Oil Challah,
    205–7
tempeh, 19, 154
    Tempeh and Artichoke
    "Marbella," 129
    Tempeh and Bean Cholent, 155
tofu
    choosing, 41
    draining, 41
    Lemony Blintzes, 56–57
    as protein source, 19
    Savory Pulled Mushroom and
    Tofu "Brisket," 122
    Sesame Tofu "Schnitzel," 126
    silken, as egg substitute, 24
    Za'atar and Feta Khachapuri,
    170–71

tomatoes
    Chickpea and Olive Shakshuka,
    169
    Confit Tomato, Garlic, and White
    Beans with Zhoug, 174
    Everything Bagel "Fattoush"
    Salad with Za'atar Cheeseballs,
    88
    Hearty Lentil Goulash, 152
    Horseradish Bloody Mary, 228
    Kasha and Mushroom Cabbage
    Rolls, 133–35
    Pizza Challah, 211
    Sabich Grain Bowl with Crispy
    Chickpeas, 158–59
    Spiced Cauliflower Chraime, 143
    Sweet and Sour Cabbage Soup, 74
    Tempeh and Bean Cholent, 155
toum, 38
    Garlic Toum, 240
turmeric
    Turmeric Matzo, 222
    Turmeric Vegetable Matzo Ball
    Soup, 83
tzimmes, 38, 109
    Carrot and Parsnip Tzimmes with
    Dates and Pecans, 108

U

Unicorn Challah, 211

V

vareniki, 132
    Sweet Potato and Sage Vareniki
    with Hazelnuts, 130–32
vegetables
    Chickpea Noodle Vegetable Soup,
    70
    Refrigerated Pickled Everything,
    236
    Turmeric Vegetable Matzo Ball
    Soup, 83
    washing, 42
    See also individual vegetables
vegetarian diet, transitioning to, 25
vermouth
    Olive and Sumac Martini, 227
vodka
    Date Syrup and Hawaij Espresso
    Martini, 231
    Horseradish Bloody Mary, 228
    Olive and Sumac Martini, 227

W

walnuts
    Apple and Honey Porridge Bowl,
    54
    Apple and Pear Charoset, 242
    Kasha and Mushroom Cabbage
    Rolls, 133–35
    Matzo Olive Oil Granola, 63
Whipped Cream, 201
whiskey
    Apple and Honey Whiskey Sour,
    227
    New York Sour with Red Wine
    and Pomegranate Molasses,
    229
"Whitefish" Salad, Heart of Palm, 51
wine
    Manischewitz, 241
    Manischewitz Blueberry
    Compote, 241
    Mulled Manischewitz, 229
    New York Sour with Red Wine
    and Pomegranate Molasses,
    229
    Pomegranate Red Wine Spritzer,
    226
    Red Wine–Braised Beets with
    Creamy Mamaliga, 144

Y

yeast
    freshness of, 42
    nutritional, 19
    storing, 42
Yiddish, 38
yogurt, vegan, 22
Yom Kippur, 31, 52, 58
Yossi's Lemony Lentil Soup, 77

Z

za'atar, 38
    Za'atar and Feta Khachapuri,
    170–71
zhoug (zhug), 38
    Confit Tomato, Garlic, and White
    Beans with Zhoug, 174
    making, 239
    Smooth and Creamy Hummus,
    Four Ways, 119
zucchini. See squash

Conversion Tables

Liquid Measures

QUART	PINT	CUP	LITERS	MILLILITERS
2	4	8	2	2000
1	2	4	1	1000
½	1	2	½	500
¼	½	1	¼	250

FARENHEIT	CELSIUS
100	35
105	40
115	45
120	50
150	65
175	80
200	95
225	110
250	120
275	135
300	150
325	165
350	180
375	190
400	200
425	220
450	230
475	240
500	260
550	290

Dry Measures

CUPS	TABLESPOONS	TEASPOONS	GRAMS
1	16	48	229
¾	12	36	170
⅔	10	32	152
½	8	24	114
⅓	5 + 1 teaspoon	16	57
¼	4	12	29
⅛	2	6	14

TABLESPOON	TEASPOON	ml
1	3	15
½	1½	7.5
	1	5

Acknowledgments

This book would never have been possible without the support and love of the incredibly special people in my life

First and foremost, to my husband and best friend, Joshua Siva. Thank you for always encouraging me to reach higher throughout my career. Thank you for being my taste tester, dishwasher, business manager, sounding board, proofreader, shoulder to cry on, and biggest cheerleader. Without you, I would never have dreamed that this was possible or dared to try. You've been my anchor. Thank you for your endless encouragement throughout this process. Without your support, I would never have believed that I could achieve this. From late-night dishes, tech support, and proofreading, I am so grateful for you and the family we have created.

To my little Ari. This book, all my work, and the rest of my days are for you. I hope that you share my love and passion for food, community, and Jewish traditions.

To my loving parents, Alyson and Barry, for always encouraging me to pursue my dreams and supporting my unconventional career. For giving me space to become who I am, make mistakes, and for always lending a hand and cleaning up after me. I am so blessed to have you as both role models and supporters. Thank you for instilling the value of family, independence, and Jewish pride in me.

To my family and friends, there's no me without you. You have provided me with unwavering support, being patient when I obsess over a tiny detail, providing me with honest feedback and words of encouragement. From eating leftovers, helping with Buckwheat, or joining me at the dinner table, I am so grateful for you all.

To my thoughtful testers and fellow food lovers, who took time out of your hectic lives to try new recipes and provide feedback to make this book a success. You are the unsung heroes of this process.

To the team at Collective Book Studio for taking a chance on me and sharing in my vision. To my support staff, Bebe Carminato for your endless creativity, Neetu Laddha for helping me to create beautiful imagery that tells a story, and Hannah Lozano for your talent and photography skills.

And lastly, to those who raised me, and shared their love for cooking with me. To my grandparents, Arnold, Louis, Eva, and Muriel. Because of you, this book exists, and with any luck, we can continue to raise generations of proud Jewish people.

About the Author

Micah Siva is a trained chef, registered dietitian, recipe writer, and food photographer, specializing in modern Jewish cuisine. After graduating from the Natural Gourmet Institute of Health & Culinary Arts, she pursued a career in nutrition and later worked for global brands, media outlets, and publications in food media. She shares Jewish-inspired, plant-forward recipes through her blog, *Nosh with Micah*. Micah lives in San Francisco, California, with her husband, Josh; son, Ari; and their mini sheepadoodle, Buckwheat.